Mountaineering First Aid

Mountaineering
First Aid

mountaineers
outdoor
basics

**A Guide to
Accident Response
and First Aid Care**

FIFTH EDITION

Jan D. Carline
Martha J. Lentz
Steven C. Macdonald

THE MOUNTAINEERS BOOKS

THE MOUNTAINEERS BOOKS
is the nonprofit publishing arm of The Mountaineers Club,
an organization founded in 1906 and dedicated to the exploration,
preservation, and enjoyment of outdoor and wilderness areas.

1001 SW Klickitat Way, Suite 201, Seattle, WA 98134

© 1972, 1975, 1985, 1990, 1996, 2004 by The Mountaineers Books

First edition, 1972. Second edition, 1975. Third edition, 1985; revised 1990. Fourth edition, 1996. Fifth edition, 2004

Published simultaneously in Great Britain by Cordee, 3a DeMontfort Street, Leicester, England, LE1 7HD

Manufactured in Canada

Project Editor: Margaret Sullivan
Copyeditor: Paula Thurman
Cover and Book Design: The Mountaineers Books
Layout: Mayumi Thompson
Illustrator: Bob Cram and Hans Neuhart/Electronic Illustrators Group

Cover photograph © Nancy Duncan-Cashman

Library of Congress Cataloging-in-Publication Data
Carline, Jan D.
   Mountaineering first aid : a guide to accident response and first aid care / Jan D. Carline, Martha J. Lentz, Steven C. Macdonald.— 5th ed.
      p. cm.
   Includes bibliographical references and index.
   ISBN 0-89886-878-5 (pbk.)
   1. Mountaineering injuries. 2. First aid in illness and injury. I. Lentz, Martha J. II. Macdonald, Steven C. III. Title.
   RC88.9.M6C37 2004
   616.02'52'088796522—dc22
                                                     2004012711

Dedication

Clint Kelley was a chairman of The Mountaineers First Aid Committee, an American Red Cross instructor trainer, and an important influence in the Mountaineering Oriented First Aid Program. Of all his many activities in mountaineering and conservation, he may have made his greatest contribution to the first aid program. Clint was a mentor to a whole generation of instructors, shaping their attitudes and approaches to first aid practice. Above all, he was a gentle and joyful instructor. This book is dedicated to the memory of Clint Kelley: leader, instructor, and good friend.

Contents

Foreword

The relationship between The Mountaineers and the American Red Cross serving King and Kitsap Counties embodied in this book reaches back to 1968. At that time, these two organizations saw the need for a first aid course designed to address emergencies when medical help is not readily available. For those enjoying the mountains and wilderness, it was also important to provide training on pre-trip preparation and in-the-field, immediate first aid response.

Mountaineering Oriented First Aid (MOFA) training starts with the American Red Cross First Aid/CPR/AED course and uses the time-honored Red Cross approach of learning by doing. Expanding upon this basic curriculum, The Mountaineers have added a wealth of information and skills focused on providing care when supplies are limited to what is in your backpack or available in the natural environment. The Mountaineers have used this curriculum to train hundreds of leaders and thousands of outdoors enthusiasts since the program began. They are committed to making sure that those who enjoy our wonderful wilderness areas are prepared for emergencies.

With the publication of this edition we celebrate thirty-six years of successful partnership between our two organizations. Both The Mountaineers and the American Red Cross endorse quality training and place a very high value on preparedness. The Mountaineering Oriented First Aid Course provides outstanding training to anyone who wants to enjoy the out-of-doors and be prepared to handle emergencies. In addition, this book is an excellent companion to add to the equipment and supplies in your backpack.

Dotty Klyce
Director, Health and Safety Services
American Red Cross Serving King and Kitsap Counties

Acknowledgments

This book continues the basic philosophy of the first editions of *Mountaineering First Aid,* by Dick Mitchell. In the early 1970s, Dick and a group of Seattle Mountaineers developed the Mountaineering Oriented First Aid (MOFA) Program to fit the needs of climbers with first aid adapted to the mountaineering environment. The local chapter of the American Red Cross has provided invaluable support to MOFA from its inception. More than 500 students complete the MOFA program each year in King County. The support of our instructors, the Seattle Mountaineers, and the American Red Cross Chapter serving King and Kitsap Counties make this program possible.

The third edition of *Mountaineering First Aid* was the result of an equal collaboration of its three authors, and the order of names on the cover represented a "draw of a straw." I was the author of the fourth and fifth edition revisions. The contributions of Marty Lentz and Steve Macdonald to the third edition are a major portion of this book. Other MOFA instructors have contributed to this work, among them are Gordon Pfister, Jeff Lundt, Scott Hansen, Jon Shields, Dave Shema, Emilio Marasco, Sandy Donnelly, and Karl Brackmann. Students' requests for clarifications and new information have also shaped this book. The contributions of past authors and reviewers still exist under the new icing. While many individuals contributed their ideas and suggestions, any errors are attributable only to myself.

Finally, I would like to thank Carol Sue Ivory-Carline for her assistance in the development of illustrations, her suggestions based on her experiences teaching students and preparing new instructors for the MOFA program, and for keeping food in the kitchen while I was typing on the computer.

Jan Carline

Introduction

This book is based on good first aid practices adapted and expanded to fit the needs of a wilderness environment. It continues the successful philosophy of first aid care included in the Seven Steps for First Aid Response as found in all editions of this book.

WHAT'S NEW IN THE FIFTH EDITION?

Every section of the fourth edition has been reviewed and revised to meet the most recent standards of first aid care from the American Red Cross and Wilderness Medical Society. Updated content has been added to almost every section, including new material on the prevention of infection, splinting, and high altitude problems. New diagrams have been added and old diagrams have been revised and redrawn to improve their clarity.

Several features have been designed to allow the reader quick access to specific information about illness or injuries and first aid care. Summary boxes, which are doubled in this edition, include specific information needed to identify illnesses and provide step-by-step treatments. A new Injury and Illness Quick Reference Guide is found in the front of the book to direct the reader quickly to major sections of the book on illnesses and injuries. Cross-references in the text and an extensive index have greatly improved access to important material.

This is a first aid book. This book is not about the practice of medicine, and it does not include procedures that require advanced training and licensure. It does not include the use of special equipment carried by professional rescuers.

The authors and publisher offer in good faith the information regarding mountaineering first aid skills and prevention of illness as described in this book. This information is not intended as a substitute for a first aid course and for practical experience, which provide the opportunity to develop the skills and judgment needed for administering first aid wisely. Readers should also be aware that the information and first aid skills provided in this book are intended for use in the contexts described. The authors and publisher disclaim any liability for injuries that may result from the use of this information, correct or otherwise.

INJURY QUICK REFERENCE GUIDE

ILLNESS QUICK REFERENCE GUIDE

Before Going into the Mountains

When an injury occurs in the mountains, a first aider encounters a situation very different from that in a city. In the city, telephones, ambulances, and advanced medical help are only minutes away. In the mountains, just getting to a phone may require hours of difficult travel. Getting outside help to the injured requires even more time, sometimes days. Cellular phones and radios can speed up the contacting of rescuers but may not work in rugged terrain or great distances from urban areas. It still may take hours for a rescue party to reach the trailhead after authorities have been contacted. Rather than being responsible for the care of the patient for a few minutes, the mountaineering first aider will need to provide care for hours or days.

The time needed to get the injured to medical care multiplies the responsibilities of the first aider. For example, contact lenses left in place on an unconscious patient will, after a number of hours, cause damage to the surface of the eyes. In the city, where the patient can be quickly taken to a hospital, eye care is provided by hospital staff. In the mountains, the responsibility to detect and remove the contact lenses falls on the first aider.

The harsh mountain environment can pose a threat to healthy and strong persons, to say nothing of someone who is injured or ill. Exposure to heat, cold, high altitude, and inclement weather can cause problems infrequently encountered in the city. Keeping a patient warm is much more difficult on a snowy mountain slope than in a heated building. Storms, avalanches, and rockfall pose additional threats to the injured as well as to the first aider.

The problems of providing first aid in an extreme environment are made even more difficult by lack of equipment. All the first aider will have to work with is what the party carried in with them. Selecting and packing equipment before leaving home must be done with the knowledge of some of the special problems associated with first aid in the mountains.

This book provides basic information needed for first aid and prevention of illnesses in the mountains. Chapters 1 and 2 describe the environment in which mountaineering first aid takes place and discuss a basic approach to first aid response, known as the Seven Steps. These steps help ensure that all responses that are needed for successful first aid can be applied in the confusing and potentially frightening situation of an accident. Important material has been highlighted by the use of numbers, bullet points, and boxes. If actions need to be carried out in a specific order, they are numbered. If the actions do not need to be performed in a particular order, bullet points have been used. Summaries of basic information and principles of first aid care are found in boxes. First aid information for many specific injuries and illnesses is found in Chapter 3. Chapters 4 and 5 discuss the two remaining steps of first aid response that focus on the skills of planning and carrying out a complex first aid response.

DEFINING FIRST AID: CARING FOR THE PERSON WHO HAS BEEN HURT

First aid is defined as "the immediate care given to a person who has been injured or suddenly taken ill." To you, as a first aider, this means two very important things:

- The first aid you perform must be **immediate.** In some cases you should take action in less than a minute. In other cases, the most important immediate action will be to simply observe the scene and talk with the patient and party members. The initial information you obtain will be critical in determining the appropriate first aid response. The information gained from these immediate observations will direct the care to be given minutes or even hours after an accident has occurred.
- First aid is the immediate **care** given. This care includes not only bandaging or splinting the patient's physical injuries and protecting them from the environment but also caring

for the patient's entire mental and physical being. A wound is more than just bleeding. It involves pain, concern, anxiety, worry, and apprehension. All of these mental and emotional as well as physical needs must be attended to by the first aider.

Nearly all injured people want help. They want to know they will be all right; they want reassurance. This does not mean you should lie to them. It does mean they want the assurance of knowing someone qualified is there to help. They want to know the seriousness of their injuries and what the first aider plans to do. In short, they usually want someone to talk to. This serves the first aider's needs too, since it enables him or her to determine how well the care given is working (does that make it hurt less?) and relieves the first aider's apprehension. This process, talking and attending to the patient's emotional needs, is called Tender Loving Care (TLC). TLC includes keeping the patient warm, comfortable, fed, busy, interested, happy, confident . . . and brave, and reverent, if applicable. TLC is extremely important, being one of the most effective remedies a first aider can provide. TLC requires no special equipment; it is always available, even in remote areas, wherever there is a concerned rescuer. Its use cannot be overemphasized.

Mountaineering first aid includes two additional but equally important dimensions:

- Because medical care and evacuation may be delayed for hours or days, mountaineering first aid includes the knowledge and skills needed to maintain the life and well-being of patients and party members until help arrives.
- Many accidents and illnesses can be prevented by knowing the causes of environmentally related diseases, for example, hypothermia and snowblindness, and using this information to guide practice in using gear, drinking sufficient water, and maintaining food intake.

This book includes important information you will need to prevent many illnesses. Other outdoor knowledge and skills, such as the selection of clothing and other gear, although not included in this book, are critical to safe travel in the mountains.

CAUSES AND PREVENTION OF INJURIES

For over thirty years, the American Alpine Club has been publishing the annual report of its Safety Committee as a booklet entitled *Accidents in North American Mountaineering*. It is a sobering account of serious injuries and sudden illnesses that befall mountaineers, with analyses of specific incidents and statistics on deaths, injuries, and causes. On average, thirty-five climbers are reported killed in the United States each year, with another hundred injured, not including skiing or hiking accidents.

There is a difference between accidents and injuries: an accident is an incident, or event; an injury involves harm to the body. The prevention of injuries includes consideration of both the causes of accidents and the causes of injuries.

Mountaineering injuries result from one of three circumstances: a climber falling (on rock or into a crevasse); something falling on a climber (rocks, avalanche); or the effects of some environmental extreme (such as cold or high altitude). A variety of factors can cause accidents, ranging from judgmental error (such as exceeding one's abilities) to simple failure of equipment. These factors can be called "contributory" causes: they contribute to an accident, but they do not in themselves cause an injury. The injury results from a more immediate cause, such as a fall.

The following are examples of contributing causes from the American Alpine Club's *Accidents in North American Mountaineering:*

Bad judgment using equipment:
   Climbing unroped
   Inadequate equipment/clothing
   No hard hat
   Placing no or inadequate protection

Performance/judgment error:
   Exceeding abilities
   Climbing alone
   Party separated
   Failing to follow directions

Environmental conditions:
   Bad weather
   Darkness
   Falling rock
   Avalanche

Equipment failure:
   Chock/nut pulled out
   Inadequate belay

Perhaps the term "accident" is misleading. Mountaineering injuries are not accidental in the sense of being random or totally unpredictable. As the analyses from the Safety Committee show, the causes of an injury are readily apparent when the environmental conditions and the capabilities of the climber are known. The prevention of that injury involves assuring a reasonable match between the performance of the climber and the demands of the environment.

For example, when you are in an environment where there is a high risk of injury from rocks falling on your head, wearing a climbing helmet can reduce the risk of injury. The helmet will not stop the rocks from falling, but it can prevent the rock from hurting your head. Alternatively, you can choose a route that does not expose you to rockfall. Prevention, therefore, involves either altering an immediate cause of injury (rockfall) or altering a contributory cause (not using a helmet).

Risk and Safety

Rockfall is a risk of going into the mountains. But what is safe? *Risk* is a number, a statistic, which indicates the likelihood that an event will occur. For example, out of the six thousand people who try to climb Washington State's Mount Rainier each year, an average of three people die, so the odds of death are one in two thousand. *Safety* is a judgment call, a decision about how much risk the climber is willing to accept. The decision to climb Mount Rainier may be made because the climber feels that the benefits, enjoyment, and sense of accomplishment justify the risks. For some, the sense of risk actually increases the benefit; that is, the greater the risk, the better the experience, as far as they are concerned.

People vary in their willingness to take risks. An extremely cautious person maintains a large gap between his or her capabilities and the demands imposed by the environment, you could say, a large "margin of safety." The extreme example is the person who stays home when the avalanche danger is low to moderate, rather than choosing a route along a ridge top. At the other end of the scale is the person who maintains a narrow gap between his or her capabilities and the task demands, a small "margin of safety." This would describe the person who pushes himself or herself near the point of exhaustion to bag just one more peak.

Acceptable Risk

How safe is "safe enough"? It would be impossible to totally eliminate risk. Further, willingness to take risks and challenge ourselves can be an important growth experience. The decision is to limit oneself to some "acceptable risk." The amount of risk that is acceptable for one person is not necessarily the same as that for the next person, as capabilities and desires differ. Recognizing those limits is the basis for prevention.

The limits themselves can be altered, as well. Capabilities can be improved by training, physical conditioning, and experience. It is equally important to recognize that capabilities can be reduced due to hypothermia, exhaustion, or inadequate oxygen. Protection can be increased through the proper use of equipment such as ropes, hard hats, and ice axes. The environmental hazard can be reduced by choosing a different route or waiting for better weather. Arriving at an acceptable level of risk involves maintaining an adequate margin of safety, and this requires the use of judgment.

Judgment

Judgment may mean deciding that a particular pitch requires a belay rope and the placing of protection. It may mean deciding that the summit attempt has to be postponed for today. In general, the person who routinely takes risks that exceed his or her abilities is probably "unsafe." Exceeding abilities may actually be the number one cause of mountaineering injuries.

The *Climbing Code* of The Mountaineers provides a guideline for safe practice. It includes the following:
- Carry the necessary clothing, food, and equipment at all times.
- Keep the party together and obey the leader or majority rule.
- Never climb beyond your ability and knowledge.
- Never let judgment be overruled by desire when choosing between staying with the route or turning back.

In summary, being aware of the causes of accidents will help you in preventing injuries. Both your enjoyment and your safety are best assured through setting a level of acceptable risk. Setting that level should be a conscious decision, based on sound judgment.

BEING PREPARED

A moment's thought about the mountaineering environment makes the need for advance preparation apparent. Mountains, rivers, deserts, and other areas of the wilderness do not care about people. They do not exist for our comfort or our safety. Although we may think of them as beautiful or refreshing or challenging, they are physical features, much bigger and more powerful than we are.

It is too late to begin thinking about first aid response after an injury has occurred. Some preparation must take place before ever leaving town and some must occur during the trip itself. Such advance preparation assists both in preventing injuries and in assuring that when an injury does occur, the response will be rapid and effective.

Essentials of First Aid Preparation

Mental Preparation. In order to deal with the problem of an injury or sudden illness in this unsympathetic environment, you need to have a working knowledge of first aid. You must be able to organize a first aid response and apply it to the situation at hand. Adequate planning also includes choosing a leader, discussing and selecting a route, checking predicted weather and trail conditions, reviewing the capability of the party members, and deciding what equipment and supplies should be taken.

Physical Preparation. Physical preparation involves both general physical fitness and conditioning and the ability to perform hands-on first aid procedures. Reading a book about putting on a splint or giving CPR is a good start, but it is incomplete knowledge until the physical experience of actually doing it has been repeated often enough to master the skill.

Group Preparation. Before leaving the trailhead, party members need to be sure that they all agree on the route (especially if there are areas of possible confusion or high risk) and have divided up party equipment. The leader should identify members with first aid experience as well as members with special medical or physical problems.

During the trip, **all** party members should think of possible evacuation routes, possible bivouac points, and more generally, what they would do if someone became sick, lost, or injured. That does not mean that one has to think of nothing else (that would make for a dreary trip). All too often the opposite occurs and **no one** ever thinks about these ugly possibilities. Periodically, every party member should mentally rehearse "What would we do if . . . ?"

Material Preparation. Material preparation includes the acquisition, testing, and organizing of the equipment and supplies needed for the trip. When packing for an outing, enough supplies must be included to sustain party members under uncomfortable circumstances. Broken ankles or twisted knees have a nasty way of occurring where conditions are the worst in terms of weather and terrain. A prepared person can at least survive, even if he or she has some degree of discomfort. An unprepared one may not survive!

Each member of the group should **always** assume that an emergency bivouac will be required and pack accordingly. This does not mean that everyone need carry a sleeping bag, a stove, and a tent. Each party member should, however, have enough equipment to survive the night under the worst conditions for that time of year and locality. For example, if the trip is limited to trail hiking in a low, forested, summer environment with a 48-hour forecast of clear and mild weather, then emergency bivouac equipment might include only some extra food and clothing. The party could easily survive if an overnight stay were necessary. Note that the word is "survive," not "enjoy," the night. If the weather were to become wet or cold, then more than this minimal amount of equipment would be needed.

PREPARATION FOR A FIRST AID RESPONSE	
Mental	Working knowledge of first aid
	Ability to organize and implement a first aid response
Physical	General fitness and conditioning
	Hands-on first aid skills
Group	All have mountaineering skills appropriate for the trip
	All have knowledge of the route and trip plan
	Members with first aid experience identified
	Medical or physical problems made known to leader
	Shared equipment and supplies divided between members
	All members rehearse "What would we do if . . . ?"
Material	Equipment and supplies appropriate for the trip
	Equipment and supplies needed to survive an emergency bivouac
	A few "extra" items that could be used by a sick or injured patient.

Every individual must choose how much discomfort he or she is prepared to endure. The party member who is always ill-prepared and borrows from others is not appreciated. Each member must not only prepare for the worst when packing but also prepare for the event that care will be given to others. **It is a responsibility of each party member to carry along a few additional items in excess of**

personal need that could be given to a person overcome by an injury or sudden illness. There is a tendency to withhold the donation of personal equipment to a patient, particularly under inclement weather conditions. It comes from a feeling, with good justification, that the donor might need it later. Therefore, each member must feel that there are articles in the pack in **excess** of personal needs.

The Ten Essentials

A number of years ago, The Mountaineers developed a list of "Ten Essentials." These are the basic items that **everyone** should have on **every** backcountry trip. They include the following:

- Navigation: Map of the area and compass and the skills to use them
- Sun protection: Sunglasses and sunscreen
- Insulation: Extra clothing, including raingear
- Flashlight with extra batteries and bulb
- First aid supplies
- Fire: Candle or other fire starter and matches in a waterproof container
- Repair kit and tools including a pocketknife
- Nutrition: Extra food
- Hydration: Extra water
- Emergency Shelter: Tube shelter or emergency blanket or bivouac sack and ground insulation—either sitting or sleeping pad

Other pieces of equipment are useful to the mountaineer and might be carried regularly. Signaling devices, such as whistles and mirrors may be useful. Cellular phones and handheld radios are increasingly being carried and have been used to shave hours off time needed for evacuations. Both phones and radios have severe limitations in the wilderness and should not be relied upon instead of common sense and good mountaineering skills. (Cellular phones and radios are discussed in Chapter 5.) A good insect repellent and water treatment gear might also be considered essentials in light of the increasing incidence of illness from insect bites and microbial infections (see pages 135 and 140).

In special environments, such as on snow or glaciers, additional equipment is essential, including a shovel, a stove with fuel, a pan and cover, avalanche cord and/or a radio beacon, and a rescue pulley.

None of these materials will do the slightest good if: they are not used (I don't need a flashlight, I have eyes like a . . . CRUNCH!

TUMBLE! SPLAT!); you don't know how to use them correctly (does the compass point toward or away from camp?); or you didn't remember to bring them.

The Mountaineering First Aid Kit

Many people have a false sense of security with a first aid kit. A kit is not a magic device that cures all ills. Without the knowledge of what to use or when to use it, the items in a kit are useless. This can be especially true when using a commercially prepackaged kit. A competent first aider should be able to perform a great number of first aid procedures with no more equipment than two bare hands and gear normally found in any hiker's pack. The first aid kit contains a few additional specialized materials unique to first aid needs.

The kit should be small and compact yet contain all necessary materials. It should be light, easily packed, sturdy, and waterproof. A coated nylon stuff bag seems ideal until one wishes to get at something in the bottom. A plastic box with a tight lid makes a good container, but may not store as well as a bag. A metal box can be used, and in an emergency could be used to melt snow or warm water. But metal makes it heavier. Any first aid kit is a collection of compromises. Probably no two experts will pack exactly alike, and some will pack differently over time. When selecting or assembling a first aid kit, consider the following general guidelines:

- Ensure that there is enough bulk to absorb a significant quantity of blood. Severely bleeding wounds are a common type of injury and absorbent material cannot be readily improvised.
- Wrap supplies in plastic so that unused materials are not damaged if the kit is opened in the rain. Some materials, such as bandages and bulky dressings for stopping bleeding, may be packaged separately and kept in a place that can be quickly accessed when an accident occurs. Make sure that the kit can be readily found.
- Consider the area you are traveling into and pack accordingly. If traveling on a glacier where there are no trees and ice axes cannot be spared, a wire splint would be extremely valuable if a fracture occurs.
- *Metal splints* are of several types. One is a flexible aluminum splint, a Sam Splint, made of a thin sheet of aluminum covered on both sides by foam rubber. When molded in place, the aluminum makes an excellent rigid splint.

Another type is made of stiff wire welded into a rigid shape and is known as a "ladder splint." Both these splints are versatile, useful for splinting virtually any fracture of the upper or lower extremities. The aluminum-foam and ladder splints can be found in outdoor gear shops or through medical or ambulance supply outlets. A third type is made of lightweight wire, similar to "hardware cloth" available at hardware stores. Its value is minimal for all but the smallest of fractures.

- Avoid carrying prescription drugs. If you need something for your personal use, consult your family physician for an explanation of its limitations, dangers, and directions for use. If you give medication to someone else, then you are practicing medicine (without a license). What happens if the patient is that one person in one hundred thousand who is allergic to that particular drug or your pain medication causes a climber with a head injury to stop breathing? No matter how severe the pain or your need to "do something," it is very strongly recommended that you not share prescription medication.

- A few nonprescription drugs, such as aspirin or ibuprofen, are helpful in first aid and may be offered by first aiders without advanced training. Reasonable amounts of these drugs, such as the number of pills needed for standard doses for a 24-hour period, may be carried. Each first aider should be aware of the contraindications for use of these drugs listed by the manufacturers. For example, aspirin should not be given to children, nor should adults take aspirin and ibuprofen at the same time.

- Carry first aid and rescue directions. Since no one's memory is perfect, carry a small booklet of information on what first aid to perform for various injuries or what rescue techniques to initiate.

- Carry first aid report forms and a pencil. The first aid report form included in this book serves as a checklist to ensure that the patient's condition has been completely evaluated and that those going for help have correct and accurate information. It allows you to collect information while it is available and readily remembered. Trusting only to memory, you may inaccurately recall vital signs, injuries, times, locations, and so on.

With these thoughts in mind, the following specific items are recommended as minimum contents of a kit.

RECOMMENDED CONTENTS OF FIRST AID KIT

ITEM	QUANTITY AND SIZE	USE
Adhesive bandages	6 1" x 3"	minor wounds
Accident report forms and pencil	2	document injuries
Sterile gauze pads	4 4" x 4"	wound dressings
Non-adherent sterile dressings (such as Telfa, Easy-Release)	2 4" x 4"	abrasions, burns
Bulky, absorbent dressing	4 sanitary napkins or 1 Bloodstopper	severe bleeding
Cloth-based adhesive tape	1" wide roll	multiple uses
Self-adherent gauze roller bandage (such as Kerlix, Kling)	2 rolls, 3" x 5 yards	holding dressings on
Butterfly bandages or wound closure strips	5 various sizes	minor lacerations
Transparent dressing (such as Tegaderm, Opsite)	2 sheets	cover small wounds, abrasions
Antibiotic cream	1 tube	wounds, burns
Triangular bandage*	2 36" x 36" x 52"	sling, cravat
Safety pins	3	bandage, sling
Elastic bandage	1 3" wide	sprains
Tincture of benzoin (optional)	1/2 ounce	adhesive to secure bandages
Moleskin/molefoam	4 4" x 6" square	blisters
Povidone iodine swabs	2 packages	antiseptic
Alcohol or soap pads	3 packages	cleanse skin
Sugar packets	4 packages	diabetes
Aspirin	6 325 mg tablets	headache, pain
Acetaminophen	6 325 mg tablets	headache, pain: use for children or individuals allergic to aspirin

RECOMMENDED CONTENTS OF FIRST AID KIT (CONT.)

ITEM	QUANTITY AND SIZE	USE
Diphenhydramine	12 25 mg tablets	allergic reactions
Ibuprofen	8 200 mg tablets	relieve pain
Barrier gloves made of nitrile, latex, or other materials**	2 pair	barrier against infection
Plastic bag	1 12" x 18"	hold contaminated materials
CPR breathing barrier	1	rescue breathing
Splinter tweezers	1	embedded object, tick, or stinger removal
Digital thermometer (optional)	90°F to 110°F (30°C to 42°C)	estimate body temperature, monitor water temperature

Miscellaneous useful items: antacids, Sam Splint, scissors, and several coins for a phone call. Prescription drugs for your personal use should be clearly labeled with their names, expiration dates, and directions for administration.

* Use old sheets or other dimensionally stable material to make triangular bandages. Triangular bandages made of gauzelike material may stretch and result in unwanted changes to the bandage after it is in place. Triangular bandages of coated plastic are difficult to tie and frequently come loose.

** Some individuals, particularly those who have worked in health care settings, have developed allergies to latex. Gloves are available in other materials that do not cause allergic reactions but still provide barriers to infectious agents.

When an Injury Occurs

SEVEN STEPS FOR FIRST AID RESPONSE

When an accident occurs, suddenly many tasks need to be accomplished. Some tasks must be carried out immediately, while others must wait until the accident is better understood. The Seven Steps for First Aid Response provide, in order of priority, an outline of the tasks to be completed in any accident situation. Each of the steps listed below is discussed in detail in later sections.

Step 1: Take Charge of the Situation. Objective: Get the party under control for maximum group response in a minimum amount of time. The designated leader must take charge of the situation immediately, develop an initial assessment of the accident scene, organize required activities, and assign individuals to do specific tasks. If no leader has previously been agreed upon, then someone must become the self-appointed leader and assume these responsibilities. Other party members must become good followers.

Step 2: Approach the Patient Safely. Objective: Avoid further injury to the patient and keep all party members safe. Approach to the patient must be rapid but safe. It is important to prevent further harm to the patient caused by rockfall, avalanche, or falling rescuers as well as to prevent injury to the rest of the party.

Step 3: Perform Emergency Rescue and Urgent First Aid. Objective: Treat conditions that can cause loss of life within a few minutes. In a few instances, immediate rescue may be the most urgent care the first aider can provide. If the patient is in an area of high risk for snow or rock avalanche or extreme lightning danger, quickly move him or her to a safer location. **Do not move** the patient again until Step 7. The patient must be checked for breathing, pulse, or severe bleeding, and be treated as necessary, focusing only on these immediate threats to life.

Step 4: Protect the Patient. Objective: Reduce physical and emotional demands on the patient. Whatever the extent of the injuries, the patient will require protection from the environment, either hot or cold. **Do not move** the patient to end exposure to heat or cold during this step, but provide shelter from above. Talk to the patient, explaining who you are, what you are doing, and what you are planning to do. TLC is important in reducing the emotional demands to which the patient must respond.

Step 5: Check for Other Injuries. Objective: Identify **all** injuries, major and minor. Once the life-threatening emergencies have been identified and controlled, the patient can be examined in more detail. Be extremely thorough.

Step 6: Plan What to Do. Objective: Organize activities so that maximum treatment is provided with minimum cost to both the patient and the party. After urgently needed first aid has been given, initial protection from the environment has been provided, and all the patient's injuries have been identified, time should be spent planning what further tasks must be done. The leader must evaluate the patient's injuries, the party size and physical condition, terrain, weather, and the party's location with respect to outside assistance. In short, the situation needs cool analysis and development of a comprehensive plan of action.

Step 7: Carry Out the Plan. Objective: Accomplish treatment of the patient, and ensure the safety and well-being of the other party members. After a complete examination of the entire accident situation and development of a course of action, the party is ready to carry out its plan. If the plan is for self-evacuation, guidance and continued observation of the patient will be needed to ensure his or her safety. If outside assistance is requested, the party should expect that it will take a minimum of 6 to 24 hours for help to arrive. Changes in the patient's condition, or changes in terrain and weather, may require altering the plan of action.

Exceptions? The Seven Steps for First Aid Response can guide you in dealing with all injuries or accidents. If you observe your hiking partner stub her toe, or a camp mate receive a minor burn from a roasted marshmallow, common sense dictates that not all the steps are followed. A full check for other injuries will not be required, and the first aid plan will be to get out a bandage or cool the burn. If you come across a patient who is injured and you did not observe the accident, or you suspect that an injury is severe, then all the steps should be followed. A

SEVEN STEPS FOR FIRST AID RESPONSE

STEP	OBJECTIVE
1: Take Charge of the Situation	Identify required activities and assign individuals to specific tasks.
2: Approach the Patient Safely	Avoid further injury to the patient and keep all party members safe.
3: Perform Emergency Rescue and Urgent First Aid	Treat conditions that can cause loss of life within a few minutes.
4: Protect the Patient	Reduce physical and emotional demands on the patient.
5: Check for Other Injuries	Identify **all** injuries, major and minor.
6: Plan What to Do	Organize activities so that maximum treatment is provided with minimum cost to both the patient and the party.
7: Carry Out the Plan	Accomplish treatment of the patient and ensure the safety and well-being of the other party members.

patient who is walking when you first see him may be asked to move to a more comfortable location, such as under a tree. Unless emergency evacuation is required, **do not move** a patient found on the ground or where the accident scene leads you to suspect a severe injury, such as finding a patient at the bottom of a cliff or slope, until Step 7.

STEP 1: TAKE CHARGE OF THE SITUATION

Taking charge is a matter of leadership. When someone is injured or is suddenly taken ill, a rapid response is often needed. These situations are upsetting to everyone involved. Even usually active and responsible persons may need guidance or directions to accomplish simple tasks. Thus, a leader is necessary to ensure that rapid and organized response occurs.

In well-planned parties, the leader of the group is clearly designated in advance. Even in small groups a leader is absolutely necessary during response to an accident. The immediate role of the leader is to take charge, assign tasks for people to do, and then manage what goes on.

Leadership

Leadership does not require expert knowledge, a lifetime of experience, or a charismatic personality. Leadership can be as simple as taking charge of the situation and then using intuition to guide decisions. It is useful to think of leadership as "managing." Management of an accident scene involves doing the following:

- Being aware of all aspects of the situation.
- Avoid becoming so focused on one particular aspect of the problem that you lose the overall picture. Remember the saying about "not seeing the forest for the trees."
- Observe and inquire. Seek out information and advice from other party members.

In a non-emergency situation, the usual leadership style is consensus, where all party members agree on a course of action. In an emergency situation, consensus is not efficient, and a leader needs to decide on some action quickly.

A good leader might never touch a patient, put on a bandage, or tie a splint. When there are multiple patients in an accident, the leader should **not** become involved with hands-on care for an individual patient unless it is absolutely necessary. A leader absorbed in applying a splint to one patient will not be able to recognize when the treatment of a second patient is going badly or notice when another rescuer is about to walk backwards into a third patient. A leader may become involved in hands-on care of a patient when an additional individual is needed to help perform a rescue safely, another rescuer is unclear about the results of a patient examination and would like a second opinion, or the rescue party has fewer members than there are injured patients. The leader should be able to direct the resources of the party to where they are needed, to collect information about all patients involved in an accident, and to ensure that Steps 2, 3, 4, and so on, are done.

Taking Charge

There are a number of ways of taking charge. The easiest is when you have been appointed leader for a particular trip. Often, however, there is no appointed leader; when an emergency occurs everyone hesitates, waiting for someone else to do something. In that situation you have three choices: (1) state the need for action; (2) offer to assume leadership; or (3) act—take the role by initiating action.

Once you have taken charge, there are different levels of management appropriate to different situations. When other members of the party have no idea what to do (because they have not taken a first aid course), assigning tasks directly may work best. If they all know what to do, allowing tasks to be done by those who step in to do them may work well.

Tasks

No matter what type of leadership structure exists, there are tasks that must be accomplished in every mountaineering first aid situation. These tasks are unvarying. What will vary is how they will be accomplished. In a large party, the leader of the first aid response will be able to delegate the tasks to a number of different people; in a small party, one person may have two or more tasks.

Initial Assessment. The first task facing the leader is developing an initial assessment of the accident scene. How many patients are there? What does the physical environment indicate; was it a climbing accident or a long fall that might involve serious fractures? Does the weather suggest hypothermia or a lightning strike? A quick assessment of the scene is essential in determining the immediate assignment of party members to help the patients. If a patient is expected to have a severe injury and the rescue party is large, two party members should be assigned: one to do the hands-on assessment of the patient and offer TLC while the second acts as a scribe to complete a first aid response form. A patient who is walking and responsive may only need the attention of one rescuer or may be uninjured and able to help with the first aid response. **No patient should be left alone.** A patient who is walking and has only minor injuries may be moved closer to other patients to allow a single rescuer to monitor more than one patient at a time.

Additional first aid tasks that must be accomplished are as follows:

- Perform hands-on care: complete the Check for Other Injuries (Step 5) and first aid treatment.
- Record findings.
- Monitor the patient: be an ever-present contact, staying with the patient constantly, listening and providing reassurance.
- Inventory and set up equipment.
- Scout the area: check for hazards, other patients, and so on.
- Go for help when necessary.

Remember, the leader's role is not to do the tasks but to ensure that they are accomplished.

Followership

Other party members must be good followers, assume responsibility for their assigned tasks willingly, and provide the leader with information about what they have accomplished or difficulties encountered. For example, in a situation with two patients and five rescuers, the leader talks with the two rescuers who have completed the Check for Other Injuries (a "leader's conference") in order to size up the situation, while the other two people stay with the patients. The wisdom of any leader's decisions is based on the quality of the information given by the followers. A good follower identifies specific actions (within the assigned task) that need to be done and accomplishes them. "Taking charge" of your own actions adds to the success of the accident response.

In summary, Step 1 of the Seven Steps is to take charge and rapidly assign tasks to people.

STEP 2: APPROACH THE PATIENT SAFELY

Approach must be rapid but safe. Do not approach the patient from directly above if a rock slide or snowslide is possible. Approach should be from the side or below. It is important to protect the patient and the rest of the party from further harm from rockfall, avalanche, or falling rescuers.

If the terrain is steep, difficult, or hazardous, keep the rest of the party back as one or two of the most qualified people approach the patient. Have the others begin to scout the area, inventory equipment, prepare a shelter, and so on, as necessary.

Those approaching the patient should be prepared with the proper equipment, particularly if the patient is perched precariously on a ledge or in a difficult location. This equipment might include slings, carabiners, rope, insulation, clothing, and first aid kits. Rescuers should not put themselves in jeopardy by neglecting usual precautions, such as placing protection and remaining attached to the rope in technical climbing situations. Individuals without technical climbing skills should not be expected to perform them during an accident response.

Another aspect of approaching safely arises when the patient has been attacked by a bear or other wild animal or bitten by a snake. Where is the animal? Is the snake dead?

One key to approaching the patient safely is the awareness that sometimes lightning does strike twice, so to speak. Rockfall often occurs twice in the same gully. Snowslides often occur one right after the other.

In summary, Step 2 of the Seven Steps is to approach the patient rapidly but safely. Prevent further harm to the patient as well as injury to the rest of the party.

STEP 3: PERFORM EMERGENCY RESCUE AND URGENT FIRST AID

There are several situations that require immediate action to prevent further injury to or death of the patient. These situations include environmental hazards requiring immediate evacuation, difficulty with or cessation of breathing, lack of circulation, and severe bleeding. Initial response requires collecting information from the scene and patient and making decisions based on the answers you find. The questions to be answered, in order, are:

1. Does the patient require emergency rescue?
2. Is the patient responsive?
3. Does the patient consent to your help?
4. Is the patient having life-threatening difficulty with breathing?
5. Does the patient have a pulse?
6. Does the patient have severe bleeding?

The answers to these questions must be determined and the required responses must be carried out in a few moments if they are to be successful.

Does the Patient Require Emergency Rescue?

Survey the scene for environmental hazards. Look around you: does the environment expose you or the patient to rockfall, avalanche, or other dangers? If the hazard immediately threatens your life, do not proceed. If the hazard threatens injury to you or the patient, perform immediate evacuation.

Rockfall, avalanche, lightning, and other environmental hazards can pose an immediate threat to patients and rescuers. These hazards may necessitate moving the patient as rapidly as possible. The leader must weigh the danger posed by the environment against the potential for harm to the patient from a hasty move. The leader must also determine the type of transfer that is best for the patient and keep the number of party members exposed to the hazard at a minimum.

Immediate evacuation. You may be able to assist a patient, who is able to walk, to move away from the hazard by providing support: have the patient place an arm around your shoulder and carefully walk away from the area. Two rescuers may provide support on either side of the patient.

If the patient cannot walk, then other methods must be used. When moving the patient, support the head, neck, and back. Keep the patient's entire body in a straight line, and avoid any twisting movement. A person can be dragged to safety by grasping his or her clothing near the shoulders, supporting the head on the rescuer's forearms, and pulling in a straight line.

Clothes Drag Rescue for Immediate Evacuation
1. Place the patient on his or her back.
2. Crouch behind the head of the patient, and grasp the patient's clothing close to the head.
3. Support the patient's head and neck by gathering clothing behind the neck.
4. Pull the patient in the direction of the long axis of the patient's body.

Patient movement during Step 3 is done to remove the patient or rescuer from immediate environmental hazard, such as avalanche or falling rocks, or to remove the patient from other immediate dangers, such as lightning or a fire. Movement is NOT done to increase patient comfort, such as moving a patient off snow or rock, or to make it easier for a rescuer to treat the patient.

Is the Patient Responsive? Does the Patient Consent to Your Help?

Check for responsiveness. Call or speak to the patient, introduce yourself, and ask "May I help?" If the patient does not respond to your question, tap the patient on the shoulder, and shout to see if the patient responds. If the patient can respond verbally, even with a moan, you know he or she is able to breathe. You cannot tell if an unresponsive patient is breathing or has a pulse without checking.

A parent or guardian must give consent for care of a child. Consent for care is assumed when a parent or guardian is not present. A semiconscious or unconscious patient is assumed to have given consent. Once consent has been obtained from a responsive patient, immediately check for severe bleeding.

CHECK FOR RESPONSIVENESS.

If the patient responds but REFUSES help: Do not proceed until consent is given. When consent is given, then proceed to check for severe bleeding. Inform the patient that you are about to check for severe bleeding and will be touching his or her body.

If the patient responds and consents to help: Proceed to check for severe bleeding. Inform the patient that you are about to check for severe bleeding and will be touching his or her body.

If the patient does NOT respond: Call for assistance from another party member, and then check for breathing.

Is the Patient Having Life-Threatening Difficulty with Breathing?

Absence of breathing or pulse may quickly result in death. Cessation of breathing or difficult breathing may be caused by lightning; crushing or suffocation by ice blocks, snow, or rock; strangulation by rope, clothing, or pack straps; falls or blows to the head; drowning; inadequate ventilation during cooking in snow caves or tents; or damage to the chest with or without an open wound. Unless immediate action is taken, the patient will most likely die within a few minutes. Removing the cause, as in suffocation, or removing the patient from the hazard, as with inadequate ventilation when cooking, may be all that is needed to restore breathing. If the patient is having difficulty breathing due to a puncture wound to the chest, seal the wound immediately, first with your hand, then with an airtight dressing (see page 80). If breathing has stopped, start rescue breathing, as described in the following section.

CHECK FOR BREATHING. If the patient is not breathing or if you can't tell because of the patient's current position, move the patient

to his or her back while supporting the head and back.

Open the airway: When there is
no reason to suspect a neck or
back injury, place the palm of one
hand on the patient's forehead, and
tilt the head back until the chin is
in a vertical position (head-tilt
chin-lift). Place the tips of the fingers of the other hand under the
bony part of the patient's chin, and
lift the jaw up and forward.

When there is reason to suspect
a neck or back injury, use the jaw
thrust method. Place your hands
on each side of the patient's head,
with your thumbs on the cheek-
bones and fingers on the back of
the jaw, push the jaw up and forward. **Do not** tilt the head back.

Check for breathing: With the air-
way held open by the head-tilt and chin-lift, turn your head so you can
see the patient's chest and abdomen and place your ear and cheek next to
the patient's nose and mouth. Look, listen, and feel for about 5 seconds.

- **Look** for movement of the chest and abdomen.
- **Listen** for the sound of air movement.
- **Feel** for air movement against the side of your cheek.
- If you see the chest and abdomen moving without hearing or
  feeling air movement, the patient is trying to breathe, but the
  airway is still obstructed. Recheck the position of the head and
  jaw to make sure the airway is open.

If the patient is breathing:
Proceed to **check for severe
bleeding.** Inform the patient that
you are about to check for severe
bleeding.

**If the patient is NOT breath-
ing: Give two breaths.**

GIVE TWO BREATHS. If the
patient is not breathing, give two
full breaths:

- Pinch the patient's nose closed between your thumb and forefinger while maintaining the head tilt with your palm on the forehead. When using the jaw thrust, seal the nose with the side of your cheek.
- Take a deep breath, open your mouth wide, and make a tight seal over the patient's mouth.
- Breathe into the patient's mouth two times. As you breathe into the mouth, watch for the patient's chest to rise. Be sure to take your mouth off the patient's mouth and take a deep breath to refill your lungs between breaths. The total time to give two breaths should be 4 seconds.

If you cannot get air into the patient: Check for an obstructed airway. If you are unable to blow air into the patient's lungs, the airway may be obstructed. Reposition the patient's head and try again. If you are still unable to blow air into the patient's lungs, use the procedures for clearing an obstructed airway.

CLEARING AN OBSTRUCTED AIRWAY. If the patient is conscious but is choking and unable to speak, or if the patient is unconscious and you have opened the airway but have been unable to give two breaths, the following steps are performed until the airway is cleared.

If the patient is conscious: Give abdominal thrusts. Stand behind him or her, circling the upper abdomen with your arms placed slightly above the navel. Grasp one of your fists with the other hand, with the thumb side placed against the middle of the abdomen, and give quick upward thrusts. Continue thrusts until the airway is cleared or the patient becomes unconscious.

If the patient is unconscious:
1. Reopen the airway and attempt to give two breaths.
2. If air still will not go in, kneel beside the patient and locate the correct hand position for chest compressions by finding the notch at the lower edge of the ribcage using your hand closest to the patient's

feet. Slide your middle and index fingers up the edge of the ribcage to the notch. Place your middle finger in the notch and the index finger next to the middle finger on the chest. Place the heel of your other hand next to your index finger on the chest. Place the hand you used to locate the notch on top of your other hand, and position your shoulders so that they are directly over your hands. Lock your elbows. Compress the patient's chest straight down to a depth between 1½ and 2 inches at a rate of 100 compressions in a minute. Complete fifteen compressions.

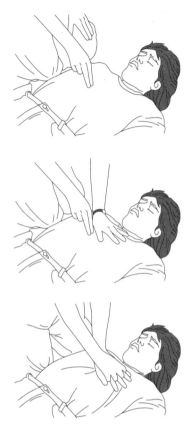

3. Check for any foreign body in the mouth. Lift the jaw and tongue with one hand. Look in the patient's mouth. If you see an object, remove it by sweeping a crooked finger along the inside of the patient's cheek and across the back of the mouth.
4. Reattempt to give two breaths to the unconscious person.
5. The above steps are repeated in sequence until the airway has been cleared. If the patient does not begin breathing when the obstruction has been cleared, check for a pulse.

Does the Patient Have a Pulse?

Absence of a pulse also quickly results in death. When there is no pulse present, cardiopulmonary resuscitation (CPR) is needed. CPR for an adult includes a cycle of fifteen chest compressions and two breaths. Chest compressions were described in the section above that deals with an unconscious patient with an obstructed airway. Complete four cycles of fifteen compressions and two breaths, and then check for respiration and pulse for 5 to 10 seconds. If there is no pulse, continue CPR. Recheck every few minutes. If there is a pulse but no breathing, continue with rescue breathing.

The procedures for effective and safe CPR are best practiced in a CPR class on special mannequins. CPR procedures are **never** practiced on another person. Taking a class in CPR procedures is highly recommended. CPR is most effective if advanced medical help is obtained within a few moments. Unfortunately, CPR may not be effective in wilderness situations when help takes hours to arrive or where the chest has been severely damaged. CPR should not be started in the wilderness if (1) the patient is breathing and has a pulse, (2) there has clearly been a lethal injury, (3) the patient's chest wall is frozen rigid, or (4) rigor mortis has begun (the patient's body has become generally rigid). CPR may be stopped if (1) the heart resumes beating, (2) the rescuers will be placed in danger by continuing, (3) more advanced care becomes available, or (4) CPR has been attempted for an extended period (approximately 30 minutes).

CHECK FOR A PULSE. Place your index and middle fingers on the patient's voice box (larynx) and then slide your fingers down the side of the patient's neck nearest to you until you have reached the space between the larynx and neck muscle. Feel for a pulse for 5 to 10 seconds.

If the patient has a pulse but is not breathing, begin rescue breathing: Give one breath every 5 seconds. Continue rescue breathing until the patient is breathing on his or her own or until you are too exhausted to continue. Visually check for severe bleeding while continuing rescue breathing. You may wish to use a breathing barrier, such as a face shield or a resuscitation mask, to reduce your exposure to the patient's saliva or other body fluids.

If the patient does NOT have a pulse and is NOT breathing, begin CPR: Rescue breathing needs to be combined with chest compressions (CPR).

Does the Patient Have Severe Bleeding?

Major wounds can cause severe bleeding. Since severe bleeding can be fatal in minutes, quick action is mandatory. The patient must have a rapid head-to-toe exam, which can be completed in only a few seconds. Arterial bleeding occurs in pulses or spurts of bright red blood. Venous bleeding is dark red and flows smoothly, without spurting. Arterial bleeding is always severe. Rapid loss of venous blood is also considered severe.

CHECK FOR SEVERE BLEEDING.

If the patient is lightly clothed (one layer of thin material), visually scan the patient for severe bleeding. Look for large areas of blood on the patient's skin, clothes, or on the ground next to the patient. Look at all areas of the body, from head to toe.

If the patient is wearing heavy clothing, do a hands-on check for severe bleeding. Starting at the head, quickly run your hands over all surfaces of the patient's body including those next to the ground. Be sure to get underneath bulky clothing and near to skin on the patient's trunk and limbs. Fluids run downhill: check to see if blood is pooling under the patient or is being absorbed into heavy clothing or being held inside rain clothes.

If severe bleeding is encountered, start treatment immediately. Don't wait to take off your pack to get out a sterile dressing. Follow the steps in the following section to control any major bleeding.

STOPPING SEVERE BLEEDING

1. Immediately apply **direct pressure** to the bleeding area. **Do not** allow severe bleeding to continue while rummaging through packs for sterile dressings or gloves. Use your bare hand if necessary. To reduce the risk of infection, use some type of barrier, such as a bandanna, between your hand and the wound. When a sterile dressing is available, place it directly over the wound. If the dressing becomes soaked with blood, place additional dressings on top of the old ones and continue to apply direct pressure. This stops the bleeding in nearly all instances. **Do not stop trying,** even if it seems to take "forever" for the bleeding to stop.

2. If the wound is on a limb, and there is no fracture of the bone, **elevate** the bleeding extremity. Elevation reduces the blood pressure in a limb slightly and will slow bleeding.

3. Once major bleeding is stopped, replace manual

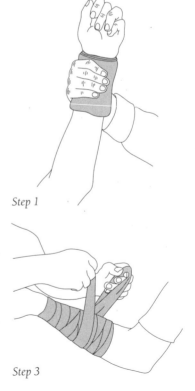

Step 1

Step 3

pressure with a snugly applied bandage. Make a *pressure bandage* by applying several bulky sterile dressings directly over the wound, then applying a roller bandage or gauze. Roll the bandage around the limb several times to hold the dressings in place, and secure the ends by tying or using adhesive tape. The bandage should be snug enough to provide pressure directly on the wound, but not so tight as to create a tourniquet by mistake.

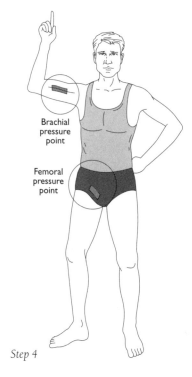

Brachial pressure point

Femoral pressure point

Step 4

4. If bleeding cannot be stopped by direct pressure alone, use **pressure points.** Anywhere that an artery can be felt pulsing as it passes over a bone is a potential pressure point. Compression at this point will reduce the flow of blood through the artery.

The pressure point in the *arm* is found at the brachial artery on the inside of the upper arm. To find this point, take the fingers of one hand and feel for the location where the two major muscles of the arm abut each other. Apply pressure by squeezing the patient's arm between your fingers and thumb.

The pressure point in the *leg* is found at the femoral artery in the groin as it passes over the pelvis. Locate the femoral artery in the crease where the leg joins the body. Press the artery against the underlying bone with the heel of the hand.

5. Once the bleeding has stopped, check for a pulse below the site of the injury or use the *capillary refill test* to ensure that circulation is maintained. Place pressure on a fingernail or toenail so that the pink color blanches (turns white). Blanching indicates that blood has been forced out of the nail bed. Once pressure has been released, the color should return within 2 or 3 seconds. Compare the speed in which color returns to a nail bed on an uninjured limb. A slow or absent return of color may indicate restricted blood flow in

the limb. If circulation is absent or poor below the injury, loosen the bandage and recheck the pulse or capillary refill.

6. Wash your hands as soon as possible after dealing with a wound. Wash your hands before touching another patient.

STOPPING SEVERE BLEEDING

1. Apply direct pressure. Use your bare hand if necessary. Place a sterile dressing directly on the wound. **Do not** remove soaked dressings. Place new ones on top of the old.
2. Elevate a bleeding extremity above the level of the heart.
3. Apply a pressure bandage once major bleeding has stopped.
4. Use pressure points if bleeding does not stop.
5. Check for circulation below the injury once bleeding has stopped. Loosen bandages if circulation is restricted.
6. Wash your hands.

When someone is bleeding, the first aider's perception of blood loss and the length of time needed to stop the bleeding tend to become distorted. Do not become discouraged; continue the efforts to stop the bleeding until successful. If these measures fail, and the wound is on a limb, and only if the bleeding continues to be severe and life threatening, apply a tourniquet. Apply it tightly enough to stop the bleeding, and once the tourniquet is in place, leave it on—**do not** loosen it. Loosening can restart the bleeding and release toxins into the bloodstream. Tag or otherwise mark the patient to alert medical personnel that a tourniquet has been placed. Indicate the time of placement. The use of a tourniquet is practically never justified. Applying a tourniquet is a decision to **sacrifice the limb to save the life.**

Action Map for Step 3

The decisions and actions required in Step 3 can be summarized in an action map. Step 3 requires that you answer six questions about the accident scene and the patient's condition. Answers to these questions direct you through the components of Step 3. An answer to one question may result in immediately performing a task, and then going to the next question on the list. Other answers may lead you to skip a question on the list. The action map summarizes the questions, the actions that are needed to provide answers, the potential answers you might receive, and then the specific first aid to be done. Many times, the appropriate next first aid step will be to go to a specific action in the map. These questions need to be answered quickly to ensure that immediately life-threatening conditions are identified and that actions to end these conditions are taken.

In summary, during Step 3 of the Seven Steps, the rescuer discovers any immediately life-threatening conditions and acts to end them. Patients and rescuers are evacuated from life-threatening environmental hazards. The patient's breathing and pulse are determined and rescue breathing and CPR are begun as necessary. Severe, life-threatening bleeding is stopped.

STEP 4: PROTECT THE PATIENT

Once urgently needed first aid has been completed, the patient must be protected from the stresses of the environment, further injury, and un-necessary fear or worry. When someone is injured, unusual amounts of energy are needed to maintain normal body functions. Exposure to heat or cold places additional demands on the body, which it may not be able to meet. These demands must be minimized. Even in mild weather, the patient may be losing heat. It is much easier to keep a patient warm than it is to rewarm a cold patient. The patient's head and trunk should quickly be covered with extra clothing to prevent heat loss. Insulation can be pushed under knees without lifting the patient's legs, or under any part of the patient where a gap between the ground and the body exists. Protection from precipitation is essential, as wetness can quickly drain away warmth. Use clothing from the patient's pack before you use your own. If the patient is too warm, loosen clothing and create shade with a tarp erected over the patient. **Initial protection from the elements can be done quickly and without moving the patient.**

Being cold or shivering IS NOT A SUFFICIENT REASON TO MOVE A PATIENT during Step 4. A shivering patient will not die because he or she has remained on snow or cold ground while a Check for Other Injuries (Step 5) is completed. A cold patient with a broken leg will still be cold for many minutes when moved on to an insulating pad but may also have a much more severe injury if the broken bones are forced through the skin during a hasty move. A patient will suffer much more damage from a quick move off snow if an undiscovered spinal fracture is dislodged and causes a spinal cord injury than from being cold for a few minutes. Complete a full check for injuries, make a brief plan for treatment including movement, *then* move the patient: this can be accomplished in under 10 minutes! When possible, all other first aid should be complete before a move is attempted. It may also be a good idea to practice a move with an uninjured party member before it is tried with the patient.

ACTION MAP FOR STEP 3:
PERFORM EMERGENCY RESCUE AND URGENT FIRST AID

QUESTION	ACTION
1. Does the patient require emergency rescue?	**Survey the scene** for environmental hazards
2. Is the patient responsive? 3. Does the patient consent to your help?	**Check for responsiveness:** Ask "May I help?"
4. Is the patient having life-threatening difficulty breathing?	**Check for breathing:** Open the airway Look, listen, and feel
5. Does the patient have a pulse?	**Check for pulse**
6. Does the patient have severe bleeding?	**Check for severe bleeding:** Visual scan or hands-on check

ANSWERS	FIRST AID
There are NO hazards	GO TO **Check for responsiveness**
There are hazards	Perform immediate evacuation Then GO TO **Check for responsiveness**
Patient is responsive and help is REFUSED	DO NOT proceed until consent is given
Patient is responsive and consent is given	GO TO **Check for severe bleeding**
Patient is NOT responsive	GO TO **Check for breathing**
Patient is breathing	GO TO **Check for severe bleeding**
Patient is breathing but is having great difficulty	Check for puncture wounds to the chest Cover the wound immediately Then GO TO **Check for severe bleeding**
Patient is NOT breathing	Give two breaths
If air goes in	GO TO **Check for pulse**
If air DOES NOT go in	Check for an obstructed airway Clear the airway if necessary
Once the airway is cleared	If breathing resumes, GO TO **Check for severe bleeding** If breathing DOES NOT resume, GO TO **Check for pulse**
Patient IS NOT breathing and HAS a pulse	Call for assistance Begin rescue breathing Visually scan for severe bleeding
Patient IS NOT breathing and DOES NOT have a pulse	Call for assistance Begin CPR with rescue breathing
Patient does NOT have severe bleeding	Proceed to Step 4 of First Aid Response
Patient IS bleeding severely	Stop the bleeding Then proceed to Step 4 of First Aid Response

A victim of a significant fall, an unconscious patient of trauma, or a patient with a head injury must be assumed to have sustained an injury to the back or neck and should **not be moved** until these injuries are ruled out. A patient of a minor fall or accident that you observed may be allowed to move to a more comfortable position.

Some conditions may require that movement takes place before the finish of the complete check for injuries. Emergency rescue requires immediate movement, as will the need to perform CPR and rescue breathing.

Keep rescuers away from the patient unless they are needed for the immediate care of the patient. A careless step on the patient's hand or the fall of a pack on an injured leg can quickly worsen the patient's condition. Packs or other gear should be left at the edge of the accident area to lessen the risk of tripping or falling. Care should be taken not to walk *over* the patient or to pass equipment over the patient that might be dropped.

Unnecessary fear and worry can only add to the patient's discomfort. One rescuer should be designated to communicate with the patient. A patient wants someone to talk with but will become confused and more anxious if several people are talking at the same time. Talking, attending to the patient's emotional needs (TLC), and explaining what will be done conveys a sense of caring and first aid competence. It is important to talk to an apparently unconscious patient, since he or she very well may hear you and be reassured. The early establishment of a calm and caring relationship will do much to reduce the stresses of the injury.

STEP 4: PROTECT THE PATIENT

Reduce exposure to cold, heat, and wet.
  If cold, place insulation over or under without moving the patient.
  If hot or wet weather, erect shelter over the patient.
Prevent further injury.
  DO NOT MOVE the patient.
  Avoid stepping on the patient.
  Keep equipment, packs, etc., away from the patient.
  Walk around, NOT OVER, the patient.
Reduce unnecessary fear and worry.
  Remain calm.
  Have one person communicate with the patient.
  Show concern for the individual.

In summary, Step 4 of the Seven Steps includes protecting the patient from the stresses of heat or cold, further injury, and unnecessary fear and worry. It also includes prevention of further injury related to hasty and unnecessary movement.

STEP 5: CHECK FOR OTHER INJURIES

Patient assessment begins during the first steps of first aid response with the initial observation of the accident scene in Step 1, continues with the initial rapid check in Step 3, and reaches its greatest intensity during Step 5: Check for Other Injuries. Assessment does not stop at the end of Step 5 but continues with follow-up examinations of the patient needed to identify any changes in the patient's condition as first aid and rescue efforts continue. The intent of the assessment is to:

- Identify the patient's injuries and the circumstances and events contributing to the patient's condition.
- Monitor the patient's condition until rescue is completed, so that any changes in the patient's condition can be taken into consideration.
- Provide information to rescuers and medical personnel about the nature of the patient's condition. Appropriate plans for evacuation will depend on this information.

General Principles of Check for Other Injuries

There are several general principles that should guide the check for other injuries.

Do no further harm. Do not move a body part or ask a patient to do so until injury has been ruled out. A gentle but firm touch should be used. A light brush of the hand will NOT be sufficient to discover injury.

Be complete and systematic. Examine every portion of the patient. Time is usually not a significant factor in proceeding with the examination. Do not be led astray by the obvious injury, as there may be multiple injuries.

Use direct observation. Rely on senses of vision, hearing, touch, and smell. Assume that there is an injury to a body part until you have directly observed otherwise.

Get to bare skin. It is essential to visualize the patient's skin to identify signs of potential injury. Clothing may need to be cut to observe the skin. Cut the clothing so that it can be easily folded or taped together to protect the patient. Protect the patient with a tarp or by quickly replacing clothing as one area of the body has been examined.

Observe the patient's right to privacy when removing clothing.

While it is essential to actually observe skin, the whole body need not be exposed while only a portion is being examined.

Compare body parts. Some fractures or dislocations may be indicated only by an unusual shortening of a limb. Compare one limb with another, or with a rescuer's limb, to see if a deformity, unusual movement, or unusual position is present.

Have one person do the examination. More than one set of hands on a patient at the same time may result in misleading findings, in addition to increasing the patient's anxiety.

Make multiple observations. Changes in a patient's condition can provide important information about injury when described to medical personnel and may lead to changes in plans for first aid in the field.

Record all your findings. Use a second first aider to act as a recorder. Record the time as well as the finding.

Record both signs and symptoms. Signs are observable indications of illness, such as bleeding or rapid breathing. Symptoms are the sensations reported by the patient, such as nausea or shortness of breath.

During the examination, do not give first aid other than that covered in Step 3. Treatment of other injuries or conditions should wait until the full examination is completed, all injuries have been identified, and a treatment plan devised.

Do not move the patient. A physical examination can be completed on a patient who is in a position other than on his or her back.

Components of the Check for Other Injuries

The components of Step 5, in order of completion, are listed and discussed in the following sections.

COMPONENTS OF STEP 5: CHECK FOR OTHER INJURIES

1. Initial Observations
2. Vital Signs
3. Head-to-Toe Examination
4. Repeat Vital Signs and Head-to-Toe Examination

Initial Observations

Information about the patient's condition can be gained by noting the circumstances of the accident. A long fall will probably result in greater injury than a short tumble. A fall onto rock should raise suspicion of a head, neck, or back injury. Wet, cool weather should suggest hypothermia. Quickly observing these facts can help in estimating the type and severity of injury sustained by the patient.

A patient with a minor injury, such as a stubbed toe you observed occurring in a party member on the trail in front of you, may not need to undergo a complete examination. In contrast, some patients may not be aware of their own serious injuries. Keep a high level of suspicion of the seriousness of any injury, particularly if you did not witness the accident.

When you arrive at the accident scene, introduce yourself to the patient. Give your name and an indication of your first aid training. **Ask the patient if you may help.** The patient has the right to refuse, and *you may not proceed until consent is given.* Additional explanation may help a reluctant patient to accept aid. Obtain consent from a parent or guardian before examining a child or infant. An unconscious patient is assumed to have given consent. Tell the patient what you are about to do. Even an apparently unconscious patient may be able to hear what you are saying and may be calmed by knowing what to expect.

Ask the patient: *What happened? How did it happen? When did it happen? What hurts? Do you have any other problems? Medical conditions? Allergies? Are you cold, hungry, or exhausted? Are there other members in your party?*

Information gained from a conscious patient is important in the identification of first aid needs. A patient who later becomes unconscious will not be able to answer questions. Ask similar questions of others who saw the accident or know the patient.

As you talk to the patient, observe: Is there any obvious deformity? Does the patient seem abnormally pale, sweaty, or nervous? Is the patient aware of the surroundings and able to respond reasonably to questions? Does the patient's position, such as holding onto a painful elbow or forearm, indicate the mechanism or type of injury? After these initial steps have been completed, the full patient examination may begin.

Vital Signs

Vital signs indicate the level of the body's essential functioning. Checking vital signs is an important part of an examination. Vital signs include pulse, breathing, skin color and temperature, pupil reactions, state of consciousness, sensation, and the ability to move. Normal values for the vital signs are given in the following box:

VITAL SIGNS	NORMAL VALUES
Pulse .	60–100/minute in adults, increased by exercise or fear, may be lower in athletes
Breathing	12–15 breaths/minute in adults
Skin	Underlying reddish tone; warm and dry to the touch
Pupils of the eyes	Regular in outline and the same size; contract upon exposure to light
State of consciousness	Fully alert, responsive to verbal and/or physical stimuli; aware of time, place, and location
Sensation of pain and ability to move	Reacts to stimuli and moves easily upon command

Pulse. The pulse indicates the rate at which the heart is pumping blood. The pulse can be felt at the wrist, in a hollow just back from the thumb. It may also be felt at the neck, just to the side of the larynx, and on the inside surface of the ankle just behind and below the large bony bump. Note the pulse by using the first two fingers of the hand (not the thumb); count the number of beats in 15 seconds and multiply by four. Also note the strength and regularity of the pulse.

Breathing. Rate and depth of breathing is an indication of how adequately the body is being supplied with oxygen. The difficulty or ease of breathing, its regularity, and any noises associated with breathing should be noted. Check the rate of breathing by placing a hand where the

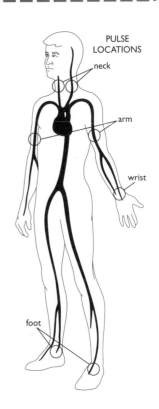

PULSE LOCATIONS

neck

arm

wrist

foot

patient's chest and abdomen meet. Count the number of movements in a minute. The presence of gurgling sounds or sputum coming from the mouth or nose should also be noted.

Skin. The skin normally has an underlying reddish tone. Absence of this tone may be seen as ashen or pale color in Caucasians, dull ashen gray in black-pigmented persons, and a dull yellowish brown in brown-pigmented persons. The skin may also appear mottled, yellowish, bluish, or pale and white. The presence of sweat and any unusual warmth or coolness should be noted.

Pupils of the Eyes. Pupil response is an indication of central nervous system functioning. Unevenness in the size of the pupils, or slow reaction of the pupils to light, may indicate serious injury to the head. Pupil response may be checked by shading the eyes with a hand, then exposing the eyes to sunlight, or by flashing a light in the eyes. Both pupils should contract promptly and evenly. Note any differences between the eyes.

State of Consciousness. The patient's state of consciousness is another indication of central nervous system functioning. Any departure from normal alertness should be noted, such as combativeness or confusion. The patient should be able to describe recent events, such as stopping to eat in the last hour, and approximate time and location. The quality of speech, ranging from clear to slurred, may be an important sign of injury. If a patient seems unconscious, can he or she be awakened by verbal or painful stimuli?

Sensation and Movement. Lack of reaction to painful stimuli may denote damage to the nervous system. Even an unconscious patient will move away from painful stimuli if there is no paralysis of the appropriate muscles. When testing for sensation, be careful not to give cues to the patient. Ask a conscious patient, "What am I touching?" rather than, "Can you feel this on your right leg?" An anxious patient, hoping not to be injured, may mistakenly report the sense of touch when it is absent. Movement should be accomplished easily upon command. Testing for the ability to move should begin with small movements, such as wiggling the fingers or toes. Then progress to larger movements, such as grasping with the hand or pushing with the foot. The last to be tested should be movements of the full limb. If you suspect a fracture, do not request the patient to move that limb other than wiggling toes or fingers. Similarly, do not request a patient with a suspected back or neck injury to sit up or move about.

Body temperature may be considered another important vital sign. Adult body temperature, taken orally, is normally 98.6°F.

"Normal" is misleading, as body temperature varies a couple of degrees during the day, lower during sleep and higher in late afternoon. Temperature varies with level of exertion, and average temperatures can differ between individuals. Temperatures above an individual's usual level may indicate fever from infection or illness or that the individual has just run a mile in warm weather. In the first aid setting, feeling the forehead of a patient is sufficient to identify a fever. Knowing the exact temperature of a patient is probably not necessary. For illnesses in which temperature readings would be helpful, hypothermia (being too cold) and hyperthermia (being too hot), it is important to measure the temperature of the core of the body, usually via the rectum. Oral temperature does not reliably indicate body core temperature. It is fortunate that other signs and symptoms are adequate for identifying these illnesses, as a first aider is highly unlikely to take a rectal temperature on anyone but the closest of friends. If a first aider wishes to carry a thermometer, the most useful one would be an oral thermometer that can register temperatures between 90° and 105°F—used to monitor the temperature of water needed to treat frostbite.

Head-to-Toe Examination

The head-to-toe is the systematic method of assuring that every portion of the patient's body is examined so that no injury goes undiscovered. Specific indications of injury include:
- Deformity, such as abnormal length or shape of a body part, or a difference in shape between left and right side
- Bruising or other discoloration
- Bleeding or other loss of fluids
- Swelling
- Abnormal movement of a body part, such as a joint moving in an abnormal direction
- Inability to move or limited range of motion
- Lack of expected symmetry, either in appearance or function
- Pain responses: generalized pain in an area, pain at a specific point, pain on motion, pain on touch (tenderness)

Ask the conscious patient about pain or sensation in each part of the body. Ask the patient to describe the pain: Is it constant or intermittent, dull or sharp, getting better or worse? After you have asked the patient about sensation in the body part to be examined, look at the part, then touch the part, and only then ask the patient to move the part. Medical conditions or allergies may be indicated by medical alert tags on bracelets or necklaces, or found on identification cards.

Proceed with the head-to-toe examination in the following steps.

1. Check the head: face, eyes, nose, mouth, ears, and scalp.
   - **Do not move the head** in the process of examination.
   - Look for signs of bleeding or presence of other fluid.
   - Look for any asymmetry in the face or in facial movements.
   - Look for any sign of fracture or other deformity.
   - Look in the ears for fluid.
   - Look for blood in the eye or the presence of contact lenses. A contact lens can be seen by opening the lids and shining a light from the outer edge across the eye. The edge of the contact lens will be seen as the light bends across it.
   - Look in the patient's mouth for wounds, loose teeth, or other injury (ask the patient to open his or her mouth).
   - Feel for any bumps, depressions, or blood. Start at the back of the head and work to the top of the head. Then check the front of the head.
   - Have the patient follow your finger with his or her eyes. Hold your finger about 18 inches above the patient's nose. Move your finger toward the top of the patient's head and then back to the center of the face. Move your finger toward the patient's chin, then left and right ears, each time stopping at the midpoint. Note any inability to move the eye or the tendency of the eye to continue moving when your finger has stopped. Both eyes should move at the same time in the same direction.
   - Check for equality of pupil size and responsiveness to light. Shade the eyes with a hand, then expose the eyes to sunlight, or flash a light in the eyes. Both pupils should contract (become smaller) promptly and evenly. Note any differences between the eyes.
2. Check the neck, spine, and upper back.
   - **Do not move the spine** in the process of examination.
   - Look for any obvious deformity or bleeding along the neck, including abnormal position of the head with respect to the neck.
   - Feel along the spine and upper back, beginning at the top of the neck. Feel for any indication of deformity, bleeding, tenderness, or muscular spasm.
   - Look for presence of a medical alert tag.

3. Check the chest and shoulders.
   - Look for any obvious deformity or discoloration.
   - Look for any indication of wounds or bleeding.
   - Look for any abnormal motion, such as one section of the chest collapsing while the rest expands.
   - Feel for deformity over the upper shoulders and chest. Gentle pressure should be exerted on the ribs from side to side and from front to back. Note any pain response. Place the little finger side of one hand on the sternum (middle bone of the chest) and, using the other hand, press down. Note any pain response or grating sensation.
   - Listen for any abnormal sounds on respiration or for the grating sounds of broken ribs.
4. Check the abdomen and lower back.
   - Look for any obvious deformity or discoloration.
   - Look for any indication of wounds or bleeding.
   - Feel the abdomen for any indication of muscle spasm or tender areas. Imagine the surface of the abdomen divided into four sections by a line on the long axis of the body crossed at 90 degrees by another line at the navel. Press firmly with the flat part of your fingers in each of those sections of the abdomen, including areas below the belt line.
   - Feel along the spine and lower back for any indication of deformity, bleeding, tenderness, or muscular spasm.
5. Check the pelvic area.
   - Look for any obvious deformity or discoloration.
   - Look for any indication of wounds or bleeding.
   - Look for abnormal position of the leg. The leg rolling outward may indicate injury to the hip.
   - Feel for injury of the pelvic bones. Position your hands on the sides of the pelvis, and press inward on **both sides** simultaneously. Without moving your hands, press on the front of the pelvis, so that pressure is exerted front to back on **both sides** simultaneously. Note any instability, grating, or pain.
6. Check the buttocks.
   - Look for any obvious swelling or discoloration.
   - Feel for irregularities or bleeding.
7. Check upper and lower extremities.
   - Look for any obvious deformity or discoloration.
   - Look for any indication of wounds or bleeding.
   - Look for abnormal movement or position of the limbs.

- Look for lack of symmetry between limbs.
- Feel for tenderness, deformity.
- Look and feel for indication of injuries to the feet and hands and the major joints including the shoulder, elbow, hip, and knee.
- Complete the examination of one arm before moving to the next arm, similarly for each leg.
- Ask if the patient can wiggle his or her fingers. If there is no fracture of the arm, have the patient grip or push against your hand with his or her hand. Compare the strength of response of one hand with the other hand.
- Ask if the patient can wiggle his or her toes. If there is no fracture of the leg, have the patient pull upward (toward the patient's head) against your hand with his or her foot. Compare the strength of response on one side with that on the other. Have the patient push against your hand and compare the strength of one foot with the other.
- Check the pulse above and below the site of any injury to determine if blood is flowing beyond the injury.
- Check for the presence of a medical alert tag.

Repeat Vital Signs and Head-to-Toe Examination

All vital signs should be taken and recorded periodically. In the severely injured patient, vital signs should be checked every 5 minutes for the first 15 minutes. Then check them once every 15 minutes for the next hour. If the vital signs remain about the same during this hour, then they should be retaken once every hour until the patient is rescued. In a patient with a minor injury, frequent taking of vital signs may not be necessary. Any worsening of the vital signs, such as an increase in pulse or breathing rate at rest or a decreased level of consciousness, signals the first aider to repeat examination of the patient. Injuries that might have been missed or have gotten worse need to be identified, and the first aid plan altered.

Head-to-Toe Examination in an Unconscious Patient

The unconscious patient may react in some way when called by name. Even if unable to respond to a verbal command, the patient may react to a painful stimulus such as a pinch on the earlobe or deep pressure at the base of the thumbnail. The reaction may be a moan or a movement away from the painful stimulus. For an unconscious patient, these additional steps should be added to the head-to-toe examination.

- Check the patient's level of responsiveness. Call the patient's name and note any response, either movement or noise. If there is no response to verbal commands, check for a pain response by a pinch to the earlobe or deep pressure at the base of the thumbnail and note any reaction, either movement or noise.
- Observe carefully for any movement during the examination that might indicate a response to a painful injury. The response might be slow, so allow time for the patient to react.
- If contact lenses are found, remove them from the eyes and store them safely.
- Repeat the examination after 15 minutes.
- Talk to the patient and explain your actions as if the patient were conscious.

Removing Contact Lenses. Soft contact lenses are removed by grasping the lens in a pinching motion between the thumb and forefinger. Hard contact lenses can be removed by using a small, specially designed suction device, and some lens wearers carry this as part of their personal first aid kit. Another method is to separate the eyelids and use the index finger to pull outward from the outer edge of the eye. This will cause a blinking motion of the eyelid, which should pop up the hard lens. The contact lens can then be lifted off the eyeball.

In summary, in Step 5 of the Seven Steps, the major components of the Check for Other Injuries are

Initial Observations. Note the circumstances of the injury and the initial appearance of the patient. Introduce yourself to the patient, and obtain consent to proceed. Ask the patient about his or her injury.

Vital Signs. Accurate observation of the vital signs is an essential part of monitoring the patient's condition.

Head-to-Toe Examination. A systematic examination of the patient's body must be undertaken so that no injury goes undiscovered.

Repeat Vital Signs and Head-to-Toe Examination as Needed. Repeated vital signs and examinations allow the rescuer to monitor the patient's response to first aid and may uncover conditions not initially discovered.

First Aid Report Form

The complete Check for Other Injuries provides information on which to plan first aid. In order to develop a thorough first aid plan and to assist the medical personnel who will eventually receive the injured patient, this information must be recorded. A first aider's ability to remember details is usually reduced by the stress and chaos of an accident scene. Forgotten or unrecorded information about the patient is useless. Recorded information is needed by both those who are staying with the patient and those party members going out for help. The specific nature of the patient's injuries will help rescue personnel in making decisions about the type of evacuation and equipment needed. Complete information, including any changes in the patient's condition over time, must also accompany the patient when he or she is evacuated. This information will assist health care providers giving care at the trailhead or hospital. The First Aid Report Form is designed to help the first aider accurately collect and record information.

There are three sections to the form: **Start Here** to record findings of the head-to-toe examination; the **Vital Sign Record** to note results of repeated observations; and the **Rescue Request** to be carried when going out for help.

Start Here. Begin with Start Here—where else? This section guides you through initial observations, initial vital signs, and the head-to-toe examination. Record findings in the indicated places on the form, and note first aid given in the column to the right of findings. Findings not recorded immediately will likely be forgotten. Be sure to note the time of the examination.

Vital Sign Record. On the back of the Start Here section is space for recording repeated vital sign observations. Possible terms to describe the vital signs are suggested. Changes in the patient's condition over time may be noticed only if careful records are kept. Any improvement or deterioration in the vital signs may cause a change in first aid plans.

Rescue Request. Separate the completed Rescue Request and send it out if party members go for help. List what happened, what injuries were sustained, and the first aid given. On the back of the sheet, clearly describe the party's location and its plan. The party's resources should be included as well as the type of assistance needed.

Responding to the Emotionally Upset Patient and Rescuer

A patient's emotional response to an injury is an important factor in first aid. A positive attitude and will-to-survive can greatly help the patient and the rescuers deal with the stressful and frightening experience of an

FIRST AID REPORT FORM - IN CLASS VERSION

FINDINGS	FIRST	AID GIVEN	RESCUE REQUEST

Fill Out One Form Per Victim

START HERE

Airway, Breathing, Circulation

SCAN FOR URGENT INJURIES
(Chest Wounds, Severe Bleeding)

TIME OF INCIDENT		Date
AM	PM	

NATURE OF INCIDENT
FALL: — Rock — Snow — Crevasse — Avalanche
— ILLNESS   EXCESSIVE: — Heat — Cold

WHAT HAPPENED

WHERE IT HURTS

ALLERGIES, MEDICAL CONDITIONS

BRIEF DESCRIPTION OF INCIDENT

PULSE & RESPIRATIONS —— PULSE —— RESPIRATIONS

INJURIES (List most severe first)   FIRST AID GIVEN

SKIN: Color
Temperature
Moistness

PUPILS: Regular in size
Equally reactive

STATE OF CONSCIOUSNESS:

PAIN (Location)

SKIN TEMP/COLOR

STATE OF CONSCIOUSNESS

PAIN (Location)

HEAD: Scalp - Wounds
Ears, Nose - Fluid
Eyes - Pupils
Jaw - Stability
Mouth - Wounds

NECK: Wounds, Deformity

CHEST: Wounds, Deformity

ABDOMEN: Wounds, Rigidity

BACK: Wounds, Deformity

PELVIS: Stability, Pain

EXTREMITIES: Wounds, Deformity
Sensation & Movement
Pulses Below Injury

RECORD
Time
Pulse
Respiration

VICTIM'S NAME   AGE

LOOK FOR MEDICAL ID TAG

ADDRESS

VICTIM'S NAME		AGE		DATE	NOTIFY (Name)
COMPLETED BY				TIME	RELATIONSHIP PHONE

EXACT LOCATION (Include Marked Map If Possible)

QUADRANGLE: _____ SECTION: _____

AREA DESCRIPTION
TERRAIN: — GLACIER — SNOW — ROCK
— BRUSH — TIMBER — TRAIL
— FLAT — MODERATE — STEEP

ON-SITE PLANS
— Will Stay Put
— Will Evacuate to _____

Can Stay Overnight Safely: — Yes — No
On-Site Equipment: — Tent — Stove — Food
— Ground Insulation — Flare — CB Radio
LOCAL WEATHER _____

EVACUATION:
— Carry-Out — Helicopter — Lowering — Raising

EQUIPMENT: — Rigid Litter — Food — Water — Other

PARTY MEMBERS REMAINING
— Beginners — Intermediate — Experienced

NAME NOTIFY (Name) PHONE

NOTIFY: IN NATIONAL PARK: Ranger
OUTSIDE NATIONAL PARK: Sheriff/County Police
RCMP (Canada)

Record TIME	BREATHS		PULSE			PULSES BELOW INJURY	PUPILS	SKIN	STATE OF CONSCIOUS-NESS	Other
	rate	character deep shallow noisy labored	rate	character strong weak regular irregular		strong weak absent	equal round reactive to light	color temp moistness	alert confused unresponsive	pain, anxiety thirst, etc

accident. Left unattended, emotional upset can result in the obstruction of first aid efforts and can cause rescuers themselves to become upset. A few basic ideas guide the first aider's response to the upset patient.

The rescuer's response influences the patient's response. A calm, quiet approach by the rescuer frequently leads to a similar response by the patient. Speak softly and slowly. Discuss injuries in terms that are not upsetting ("You have some bleeding" rather than "Man, it's gushing"). Keep the confusion of the accident scene to a minimum. It is better for one rescuer to talk with a patient than to have several rescuers asking questions at the same time.

The rescuer must also build and maintain a sense of credibility with the patient. Respond truthfully to the patient and do not give false reassurances. Telling the patient everything is "all right" when it is clearly not all right may imply that the rescuer is not very bright or not to be trusted. Rescuers need to be aware of their own feelings and reactions to an accident in order to give their best care. Comments of "You shouldn't feel that way" or "Snap out of it" represent what the rescuer wishes. Such comments will not help the patient, nor will argument and denial of the realities of the situation. Treat the patient as you would wish to be treated, with honesty and concern.

The range of response to an injury may be wide. The patient may be quiet and slow to respond to questions or be agitated and unable to sit still. A frequent reaction is denial, a statement that a serious injury has not occurred. It is frightening to admit that you cannot move your legs or that the pain in your forearm means a broken bone. Patients frequently will experience anger about the injury, panic that rescue will come too late, and general anxiety about what will happen next or whether they will be able to get back to work on Monday. Some patients may experience waves of grief, and others may become aggressive in response to the incident. All these feelings are normal reactions to an accident. Individuals respond in different ways. Not everyone can be expected to show the same set of feelings or the same tolerance to pain or injury. Feelings may change rapidly during the course of a rescue. Your companions may have similar difficulties in dealing with their own feelings generated by the accident scene. It is important to recognize these feelings and to help the patient (and the rescuers) cope with the confusion and fright of an accident.

To help the patient deal with upsetting emotions, a rescuer can:

Give information. Introduce yourself and let the patient know what is going to be done. Respond to questions with honest answers. Share plans for further care with the patient.

Listen to the patient. Let the patient talk about his or her fears and feelings. The rescuer may need to help the patient discuss feelings. Ask "What are you thinking? How are you doing?" The rescuer may not agree with those feelings, but they should be respected. Reassurances should come only after feelings have been accepted by the rescuer. Don't say "You shouldn't be afraid." It is better to say "I can understand that you're very scared right now, but we'll try to help you through this." Speak calmly and confidently; this will help to reduce the patient's anxiety.

Stay with the patient. Do not leave a patient alone. One rescuer should be assigned to supervise a patient. If there are more patients than rescuers, assign a rescuer to several patients closely grouped together. If a patient is very anxious or gets in the way, a rescuer may need to take the patient to an isolated location.

Use touch. Holding a patient's hand or putting an arm around his or her shoulders can be very comforting. Holding a patient by the elbow may be helpful in moving the patient out of harm's way. If the patient does not want to be touched, that wish must be respected. Physical restraint is almost never necessary and may result in injury to the rescuer if the patient is violent. Use of physical force is never acceptable, unless it is necessary to prevent injury to yourself or other patients. Use touch only if you are comfortable using it: the patient may perceive your discomfort and become more upset.

Direct the patient's thought. Asking the patient for information about the incident, involving the patient in making plans for treatment, or discussing details of life "back in the city" can help the patient to engage in constructive thought and to stop reviewing the ugly details of the accident. While directing the patient's thoughts can be helpful, the rescuer must be willing to listen to the patient's concerns and feelings.

Direct the patient's activity. If the patient is able to assist, having the patient set up a tent, prepare food, or engage in any meaningful activity can help to calm the patient. The patient will begin to feel that his or her efforts are contributing to the solution of the problem.

Provide comfort. Food, drink, warmth, and protection from further injury does much to help the upset patient. A warm cup of tea is very calming.

Upset feelings cannot be "cured," but the patient and rescuers can be helped to cope with feelings and their behavior can be directed to useful activities.

RESPONDING TO THE EMOTIONALLY UPSET PATIENT

Speak calmly, softly, and slowly—use terms that are descriptive.

Have one person communicate with the patient.

Give information—tell the patient what is being done, answer honestly.

Listen to the patient's feelings and concerns.

Stay with the patient—never leave a patient alone.

Use touch—if the patient is willing.

Direct the patient's thought to constructive ideas and actions.

Direct the patient's activity—engage the patient in meaningful activity.

Provide comfort—food, drink, warmth, and protection from further injury.

Dealing with a death. Sometimes patients die, no matter how well first aid has been given, or how well the response was led. Authorities will need to be informed, and the party members should be prepared to follow their directions. Attempts to evacuate a body should not take precedence over the health and safety of the remaining patients or rescuers. If the death has occurred on an organized outing, leaders of the club or association sponsoring the trip should be informed after legal authorities have been contacted. Notes about the accident and first aid response should be carefully kept, including any First Aid Report Form. Rescuers may want to write down their memories of the incident before details are forgotten.

If a death occurs, a major responsibility of every party member is to help each other with their emotional responses to the death and to ensure that those still alive return home safe. All the recommendations for communicating with an upset patient apply to dealing with upset rescuers. A party member who appears particularly shaken by the experience should not be allowed to travel alone, either to the trailhead or from the trailhead to home.

Feelings of anxiety, guilt, and sadness may linger for a long time. Attending memorial or burial ceremonies may help to bring closure to the event. Group discussions led by counselors or individual grief counseling may be needed.

The details of Step 6 and Step 7 are described in Chapters 4 and 5. Chapter 3 discusses injuries to specific parts of the body and specific first aid actions that will be needed to make and carry out the plan.

First Aid for Specific Conditions

PREVENTING INFECTION IN THE FIRST AIDER

In rare instances, a patient may have a serious infectious illness that can be transmitted to the first aider by blood or other body fluids. Diseases could include herpes, meningitis, tuberculosis, hepatitis, and HIV. Fortunately, these diseases are rare and the chance of finding an injured person with them in the mountains is extremely low.

Transmission of these diseases can occur in three ways: (1) touching an infected person's blood or other body fluids, (2) touching objects such as bandages, dressings, or other equipment that have been contaminated by infected body fluids, (3) inhaling airborne droplets when an infected person coughs or sneezes. Preventing infection requires placing barriers between the first aider and the patient's body fluids and carefully observing personal hygiene. The following specific recommendations help to prevent transmission of disease:

- Wear disposable (single-use) barrier gloves when there is the possibility of coming in contact with blood or body fluids or objects contaminated with them.
- Dispose of soiled materials in closed plastic bags.
- Remove gloves by turning them inside out. Directions for glove removal are listed below.
- Do not reuse disposable gloves. Discard any unused gloves that appear damaged.

- Cover any cuts, scrapes, or skin irritations you have with bandages or protective clothing.
- Wash your hands with soap and water after providing care.
- Avoid touching your mouth, nose, or eyes. Avoid eating while providing care or before washing your hands.
- Change gloves and wash your hands between contacts with different patients.
- Use a breathing mask with a one-way valve when providing rescue breathing.
- See a physician if you have been splashed by body fluids in the eyes, mouth, nose, or on skin with an open wound.

Although the chance of becoming infected is very small, the devastating consequences that are the result of contracting a disease like hepatitis or HIV provides the rationale for following these precautions.

Removing Barrier Gloves

Step 1. Begin removal of first glove.
- Touching only the outside of the glove, pinch it near the wrist and pull toward the fingertips.
- DO NOT completely remove the glove from the first hand.
- The first glove is now inside out.

Step 2. Remove the second glove.
- Pinch the exterior of the second glove with the covered fingers of the first hand (Step 2a).
- Pull the second glove toward the fingertips (Step 2b).
- Remove it completely from the second hand.
- The second glove is held by the first hand.

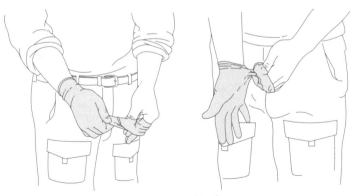

Step 1   *Step 2a*

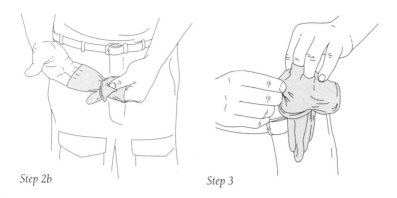

Step 2b   *Step 3*

Step 3. Finish removing the gloves.
- Using the second hand, grasp both gloves by the clean inside surface of the first glove.
- Remove both gloves and place them in a plastic bag for disposal.

INJURIES
Wounds

In mountaineering, wounds can occur in a number of ways. The cause determines the type of wound: a slip and slide on steep rock can cause abrasions; a mistake with a sharp knife can cause a laceration; stepping on someone in your crampons can cause a puncture wound (and a punch in the nose).

First Aid Goals. The priorities in wound care are first, to control bleeding; second, to prevent infection; and third, to reduce pain.

Treatment of Bleeding. The technique for stopping bleeding was covered in Step 3 of the Seven Steps. The basic methods of direct pressure, elevation, and pressure points will stop the bleeding from virtually all wounds. Placing a pressure dressing on the wound replaces direct manual pressure, from your hand, with mechanical pressure from the bandage. Check below the wound site (between the wound and the end of the limb) after the pressure dressing is in place to be certain that the circulation has not stopped in the areas beyond the dressing. Wash your hands as soon as possible to reduce the risk of being infected.

Once the bleeding is under control, **immobilize** the wounded part, using a splint if necessary. Immobilization reduces pain and prevents further movement of the wounded area, which could start the bleeding again.

Embedded Objects. Small embedded objects just below the surface of the skin should be removed, if it can be done easily with manual pressure, tweezers, or a needle.

Larger embedded objects should be stabilized in place with numerous bulky dressings around the protruding part. Removal of a deeply embedded object can cause more injury and bleeding. If large objects fall out or become dislodged during movement of the patient, the wound should be treated as any open wound.

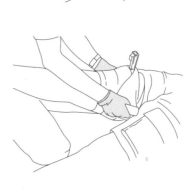

Treatment to Prevent Infection. For minor wounds where bleeding is not a severe problem or has been controlled, the wound should be cleansed and dressed under as sterile conditions as possible. The general principles of preventing infection are as follows:

1. *Wash your hands.*
2. *Use clean barrier gloves* to reduce the risk of contamination of the wound or infection of the first aider.
3. *Wash in and around the wound* to remove bacteria and other foreign matter. Any dirty wound should be washed vigorously and rinsed with large amounts of water. Pour at least a quart of water over it. Antibacterial soaps, such as those containing povidone iodine, are useful, though not absolutely necessary. Some previously recommended antiseptics, such as hydrogen peroxide or tincture of iodine, can further damage tissues and should not be used.
4. Close the wound with butterfly bandages or wound closure strips if it is gaping, but only if it is clean and small. Scalp wounds can be closed by tying strands of hair together. Use double square knots, since hair has a stubborn tendency to untie.

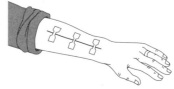

Unless you are quite certain that you have thoroughly cleansed the wound, do not attempt to close it. Small numbers of bacteria deep in the wound can make a large infection. Large gaping wounds will require evacuation for hospital care because they are difficult to clean adequately in the mountaineering setting and injury to underlying tissues will require surgical repair. Puncture wounds should NOT be pulled together, but should be left open and covered with a sterile dressing.

5. *Cover with a sterile dressing,* and *bandage.* A *dressing* is placed directly on the wound, and a *bandage* holds a dressing in place. A bandage does not need to be sterile, but a *dressing* should be sterile. Gauze pad dressings are readily available commercially. Nonadherent dressings (such as Telfa or Easy-Release pads) are particularly useful for abrasions and burns. Bandage material can be improvised (as from torn strips of clothing) or commercial. Simple *roller gauze* is cheap but difficult to use. Two-ply *self-adhering* roller bandage (such as Kerlix or Kling) or *elasticized gauze* is not as cheap but is much easier to use.

    When using tape, if the skin is cold or wet and the adhesive quality of the tape is dubious, *tincture of benzoin* may be applied to the area around the wound. Do **not** apply tincture of benzoin to the wound itself—it is used only as an adhesive to ensure that the tape will hold. Allow the benzoin to dry before applying the tape.

6. *Change the dressing every day,* replacing it with a new dry, sterile dressing. If the dressing sticks to the wound, soak it with sterile water for a few moments before removing it. Look for signs of infection: foul-smelling pus; redness around the wound, especially if extending up the limb; swelling; fever; or considerable pain, continuing longer than two to three days. Moist heat applied over an infected wound may prove beneficial, but any significant infection is cause for evacuation as soon as possible.

    Water can be sterilized by following these steps. Remove any large particles from the water by straining it through a clean cloth. Boil the water for at least 1 minute. Clean a container for the water by rinsing it with boiling water, allowing the rinse water to remain in the container for at least 1 minute. Throw out the rinse water, and place the boiled water in the prepared container. Cover the container. Water should be cooled to body temperature before use.

7. Having an up-to-date series of shots for immunization against *tetanus* is not strictly speaking a part of first aid, but it is a key part of the *prevention* of complications.

BASIC TECHNIQUE FOR PREVENTING INFECTION

1. Wash your hands.
2. Use gloves.
3. Wash in and around the wound.
4. Cover with a sterile dressing and bandage.
5. Change the dressing every day.

Eye Injury: Objects in the Eye

Getting "something in the eye" in the mountains is common. In most instances, natural watering from tears is sufficient to dislodge and wash away any object. Occasionally objects become lodged and cannot easily be removed. Rarely a large object becomes embedded in the eye.

First Aid Goals. The first aid goals are to remove small lodged objects when possible and to stabilize embedded objects in place.

Remove Objects in the Eye. Rinsing with sterile water may remove a foreign body lodged in the eye. With the patient horizontal, rinse from the nose side toward the ear. You want to avoid washing the object out of one eye into the other. The fluid should be poured into the inner corner of the eye and allowed to run over the eyeball while the lid is gently lifted by the lashes. The eye should not be rubbed. If rinsing fails, and the object can be seen, you may try to lift it out gently with a corner of a sterile gauze pad, with the patient looking away. If the object is embedded, leave it in place and bandage the eye.

Stabilize Embedded Objects. If an object is embedded in or protruding from the eye, the situation clearly is much more serious. The object needs to be stabilized in place because movement could cause fluid from the inside of the eye to be lost. Once lost, the fluid can never be replaced. Follow these steps: Place the patient on his or her back. Leave the object in place. Do not attempt to wash the eye. Place sterile

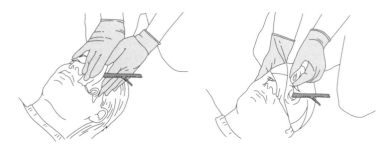

dressings around the embedded object. If the object protrudes out of the eye, stabilize it as best you can with additional dressings. Tape or bandage the dressings in place. Avoid putting pressure on the eye itself. Bandage only the affected eye. Evacuate the patient by stretcher. Under extreme conditions, such as increasing avalanche risk, it may be necessary to walk out of a hazardous area. Move slowly and attempt to prevent as much movement of the patient's head as possible. Do not allow the patient to lift or carry anything, including a pack.

FIRST AID FOR OBJECTS IN THE EYE

SMALL OBJECTS NOT EMBEDDED
1. Place the patient's head parallel to the ground, with the affected eye closest to the ground.
2. Gently lift the eyelid by the lashes.
3. Pour clean water across the eyeball until the object is washed out.
4. If the object remains, attempt to lift it out with the corner of a sterile gauze pad.

EMBEDDED OBJECTS
1. Place the patient on his or her back.
2. Leave the object in place.
3. Place sterile dressings around the embedded object.
4. Tape dressings in place. *Do not* put pressure on the eye. Bandage only the affected eye.
5. Evacuate the patient by stretcher.

Head Injury

Head injuries in the mountains are caused by objects falling on the head (rockfall, icefall, and so on), by falls in which the head strikes a hard object, or by a rapid and abrupt jerking movement to the head. All injuries to the head are potentially life threatening. Their seriousness depends on the degree of damage to the brain rather than on the visible physical damage. Bleeding from a minor scalp wound may appear to be profuse due to its location on an important part of the body. What may appear to be a lot of bleeding may not be life threatening. On the other hand, serious brain injuries can be present without obvious signs or symptoms. Assessment of severity is a challenge for the first aider.

There are two basic types of head injury: *skull fracture* and *brain injury*. They are often seen together, but it is possible to have a skull fracture without brain injury or brain injury without skull fracture. A *skull fracture* is a crack or break in the bones surrounding the brain, caused by a direct blow to the head. Although a skull fracture itself is not an immediately life-threatening injury, the possibility of brain injury should be assumed whenever there has been a blow powerful enough to crack the skull.

The brain is a large, soft organ that sits inside the rigid skull. A thin layer of fluid surrounds it. A *brain injury* can vary in severity from a fairly minor concussion to major bleeding within the skull. A concussion involves temporary loss of function of some or all parts of the brain, with results ranging from mild confusion to complete loss of consciousness. A concussion can occur directly, as in a blow to the skull, or indirectly, when the brain bounces off the inside of the skull. A very rapid deceleration, such as landing with a hard fall on the buttocks, can cause injury to the brain. *Bleeding within the skull* is the cause of significant brain injury because the accumulating blood puts pressure on the brain. An expanding blood clot will compress and injure the delicate brain tissue. Brain injuries are probably the most common cause of death in mountaineering accidents.

First Aid Goals. The priorities of first aid for head injuries are to prevent further injury, assess the seriousness of the injury, watch closely for changes, and evacuate as necessary.

Prevent Further Injury. With the head-injured patient, as with any patient, the first priorities are breathing and circulation. Follow the directions in Step 3 to open the patient's airway, check for breathing and circulation, and treat bleeding. Assuring an adequate airway in an unconscious patient with a head injury is more difficult than usual because it must be assumed that **every unconscious injured patient has a spinal injury** until proven otherwise. Approximately 15 percent of all severe head injuries are associated with a broken neck. The number-one priority is the *airway*. The jaw thrust technique may be life saving. A patient may recover if nothing is done about a spine injury, but a patient won't recover if the airway is not opened.

If the possibility of a spinal injury can be reasonably eliminated (see

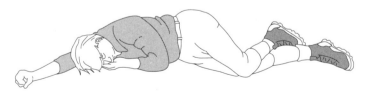

page 79 for Ruling Out a Spinal Injury), the patient may be positioned on his or her side, with the mouth pointed toward the ground and the upper leg crossed over the lower leg. This position will help maintain the airway and prevent secretions from entering the lungs.

Bleeding from a scalp wound can generally be controlled by direct pressure, although care should be used to avoid excess direct pressure on a head wound that is located over a skull fracture. These wounds should simply be covered with a bulky dressing to avoid pressing fragments of bone into the brain tissue.

Assess Seriousness. Six signs distinguish a major head injury from a minor head injury:

- *Changes in consciousness* are the most obvious signs of a severe head injury. Prolonged unconsciousness, 5 minutes or more, is a sign of serious brain injury. The length of unconsciousness is roughly proportional to the seriousness of the injury. The patient who is initially unconscious, wakes up, and then gradually becomes drowsy and loses consciousness again has a severe brain injury as well. This can occur when there is continued bleeding or swelling within the skull.

  It is reasonable to assume that a head injury is minor if the patient has not been knocked out but only is confused or disoriented for a short period of time and is now alert and oriented (knows where he or she is, the time of day, what is happening, and so on).

- Any *indentation in the skull* is a sign of a major head injury.
- *Blood or clear fluid* draining from the ears or nose is a sign of major head injury. Blood from the nose alone can result from a simple blow to the nose, so look further.
- *The appearance and function of the eyes* may be a sign of major head injury. Pupils of unequal size, pupils that respond unequally to light, or problems with the eyes in following an object are signs of brain injury. Test the movement of the eyes and function of the pupils as described in the head-to-toe examination (see page 55). The patient should be able to tell you how many fingers you are holding up in front of him or her. Difficulty with seeing may be a sign of brain injury.
- *Bruises behind the ears or around the eyes* may be a sign of major head injury.
- *A very slow pulse*, below 40 beats per minute, is a sign of a major head injury. This is unlike shock, where a rapid pulse is a sign of seriousness.

HEAD INJURY

SIGNS AND SYMPTOMS OF MINOR HEAD INJURY
Patient did not lose consciousness or was unconscious for less than 5 minutes
Patient is alert and oriented
Wounds are minor

SIGNS AND SYMPTOMS OF SEVERE HEAD INJURY
Changes in consciousness
Indentation in the skull
Blood or clear fluid draining from the ears or nose
Pupils that respond unequally
Bruises behind the ears or around the eyes
Very slow pulse

FIRST AID
Watch closely for changes for at least the first 24 hours after injury
Do not allow the injured patient to wander off alone
Take and record vital signs at least every hour
Repeat the Check for Other Injuries
Evacuate as soon as possible

ATTEMPT TO SELF-EVACUATE *IF:*
Injuries appear minor
Patient is able to walk
Terrain is safe

Watch Closely for Changes. In the mountaineering setting, a patient with a head injury might want to resume climbing after regaining consciousness. Although the patient might feel as though it is a minor injury, it is a safe rule of thumb that anyone who has been knocked unconscious should be observed closely for the next 24 hours at least, and certainly not be allowed to wander off alone. Keep a written record of the signs and symptoms you observe. Repeat your observations periodically, including the head-to-toe exam, as signs can change. Bruises, for example, may show up only gradually. Your notes might show trends of improvement or deterioration, and they could contribute to a surgeon's decision to operate within minutes of the patient's arrival at a hospital.

Evacuate as Necessary. If the patient has any of the signs or symptoms of serious head injury, then evacuation is necessary. Use the following guidelines to help you decide whether to allow the patient to walk out:

You can allow the patient to walk out with assistance (self-evacuation) if all the following points are true:

- The injuries appear minor, such as very brief unconsciousness or a small scalp wound, and there are no signs of other associated injuries, such as spine injury.
- The patient is able to walk. You can test for balance, coordination, and vision during a "trial" walk. Ask the patient to stand with eyes closed; swaying or falling may indicate injury to the brain.
- The terrain is safe. If portions of the trail require independent judgment and action (a rock traverse, for example, or steep, hard snow), where it is not possible for another party member to stay close, do not attempt walking out.

The tremendous difficulties involved in evacuating an unconscious patient from the backcountry are more than adequate justification for heading toward the trailhead while the patient is still able to walk. When self-evacuating, watch the patient closely, particularly during the first 6 hours, for signs of drowsiness, increased headache, nausea, or vomiting, which may indicate a deteriorating condition. You should send for help or evacuate as soon as possible (see pages 156–159) when the signs and symptoms indicate a major head injury. The information you send out on the first aid report form should be sufficiently detailed to allow the rescue personnel to decide how quickly they need to respond. If you are extremely close to the trailhead and you have a large, strong party, you may decide to attempt to carry the patient out. An unconscious head-injury patient is assumed to have a spine injury until proved otherwise, and thus the spine must be protected from any movement during the carry.

Prevention of Head Injuries. Severe head injuries can be significantly reduced by use of a hard protective helmet. Helmets that are made specifically for climbers are best, because they have been designed with mountaineering accidents in mind. Bicycle helmets do not protect adequately against blows to the side of the head.

Neck and Back Injuries: Damage to the Spine

The *spinal column* is a column of bones extending from the skull to the pelvis. The *spinal cord* is encased within the column, and nerves branch off of the cord to the arms, the trunk, and the legs. The cord and nerves carry sensory messages up to the brain and motor (movement) messages down from the brain. Damage to the spinal cord interrupts those messages, resulting in the inability to sense or move. A spinal fracture is a break or crack in the bones of the spinal column. These fractures can occur with or without injury to the spinal cord.

Spinal injuries can be the result of a direct blow to the spine or from a blow to the head or a fall on the buttocks (which transmits the force indirectly to the spine). Falls and falling rock are the most common causes of spinal injury in the mountains.

The most vulnerable areas of the spinal column are the neck and lower back; the upper back is somewhat strengthened by its connection to the rib cage. A spinal fracture in the neck or back causes instability, which results in less protection for the cord. Mishandling of a spinal injury can convert a spinal column fracture that has not damaged the spinal cord into one that has. The broken bone edges can easily cut into the cord. Mishandling can also convert a partially cut cord into a totally cut cord. The nerve cells in the spinal cord are almost entirely incapable of healing. Spinal damage is permanent.

Spinal injury is probably the best example of why we repeatedly say in first aid "it is better to overtreat than to undertreat." If there is any doubt about whether a spinal injury exists, assume it does and proceed accordingly. The patient who is immobilized unnecessarily suffers little harm. The patient who has a minor spinal fracture converted into a major injury through mishandling may suffer permanent paralysis.

First Aid Goals. The first aid goals for spinal injury are to assess the seriousness of the injury, prevent further injury, and monitor and evacuate.

Assess Seriousness. The patient with a neck or back injury may have sustained a fracture of the spinal column without serious injury to the spinal cord. For that reason, *any sign or symptom which is suggestive of spinal injury should be taken to mean that immobilization of the spine is necessary.* Similarly, *when the mechanism of injury* (fall, blow to the head, etc.) *suggests damage to the spine,* **immobilize** the patient. Similarly, a fall of any significant distance or a high-velocity crash should raise suspicion of spinal injury. Any trauma to the head, neck, or back should also raise suspicion of spinal injury. With the patient immobilized, repeat your observations every 20 minutes or so. The signs and symptoms may not have been obvious the first time you checked, and some patients may not develop them until later.

SIGNS AND SYMPTOMS OF SPINAL INJURY

	NECK	BACK
Symptoms		
Pain	In the neck	In the back
Numbness, tingling	Fingers, toes	Toes
Loss of sensation	Arms, legs	Legs
Signs		
Tenderness	Neck	Back
Deformity	Neck	Back
Loss of movement	Fingers, toes	Toes

The patient may report pain at the site (neck or back), numbness or tingling of the fingers or toes, or a loss of sensation. Signs that may be found include tenderness or deformity at the site (neck or back) or a loss of the ability to move the arms or legs. Carefully record the place on the body where the loss of sensation or ability to move occurs.

Check for movement of the fingers and toes and sensation as described in the Check for Other Injuries. When the injury is in the neck, both the arms and legs will be affected. When the injury is in the back, only the legs will be affected. If a change is found in one arm or one leg, the damage is usually to nerves outside the spinal column. Any sensory or motor loss, even on one side only, should be treated as a spinal injury.

TESTING FOR SENSATION AND MOVEMENT

UPPER BODY	LOWER BODY
1. Touch hand and ask: *Can you feel this? Where am I touching you?*	1. Touch foot and ask: *Can you feel this? Where am I touching you?*
2. Ask: *Can you wiggle your fingers?*	2. Ask: *Can you wiggle your toes?*
3. Have patient squeeze your hand.	3. Have patient push/pull foot against your hand.

Prevent Further Injury. When the type of accident and the symptoms or signs suggest that a spinal injury may be present, the first step

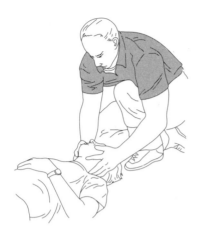

is manual immobilization of the spine: hold the patient in place so that he or she does not roll, slide, or move in any way. As with any patient, breathing and circulation take priority. If a neck injury is suspected, use the jaw thrust (see page 38) to open the airway.

With a possible broken neck, stabilize the head with in-line stabilization. Place your hands on both sides of the patient's head and gently position the head in line with the rest of the spinal cord. The hands are positioned with the index fingers just under the jaw, the thumbs on the cheeks, and the other fingers supporting the back of the neck. The palms typically cover the ears as seen in the illustration. Once hands are in place on the head, they must remain to prevent movement until more permanent stabilization is in place. A mountaineering helmet may be left in place while initially stabilizing the neck, but eventually it should be removed to ensure a complete examination of the head and to ease first aid care of the patient. Removing a helmet should be done by two people. One rescuer, with hands positioned below the helmet, holds the head and neck stable while the other rescuer removes the helmet. The rescuer who has removed the helmet then assumes the usual position for in-line stabilization. **Do not** attempt to move the patient's head in line when the patient complains of pain or pressure when you begin to move the head, or if you feel any resistance when you attempt to move the head.

The next priority is to protect the patient from heat loss or gain by placing him or her on insulation. Patients of spinal injury are particularly sensitive to changes in temperature. The patient is log-rolled (see page 153) onto the insulation keeping the neck and back in a straight line. Check the patient's skin periodically to see if he or she is getting too warm or cold.

When it is no longer necessary to move the patient, replace the manual immobilization with a method that does not require you to hold the patient constantly. The best method for a suspected neck fracture involves improvised "sandbags," filled stuff sacks or tightly rolled bulky clothing, secured around the head, neck, and shoulders.

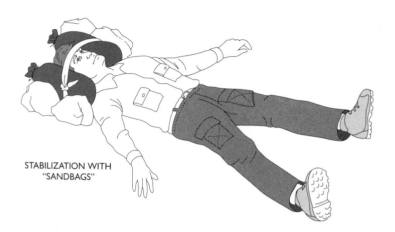

STABILIZATION WITH "SANDBAGS"

Monitor and Evacuate. Watch the patient for changes. As a result of the initial injury, many patients will have further loss in sensation or ability to move over time. Evacuation of a patient of a spinal injury must be by rigid stretcher. It is impossible to improvise a rigid stretcher with the equipment carried by most parties, so you will have to wait for an organized rescue party.

Ruling Out a Spinal Injury. You may choose to initially immobilize a patient because the type of accident suggests that a spinal injury is possible. It is safe to assume that no spinal injury is present when the patient is fully conscious and when **none** of the symptoms or signs are present (see page 77). As soon as spinal injury is ruled out, immobilization of the neck and back may be ended.

FIRST AID FOR A BACK OR NECK INJURY

Immobilize the patient with in-line stabilization and then sandbags.

Monitor and ensure breathing and circulation.

Use a jaw thrust to open the patient's airway if needed.

Remove helmet after stabilization is complete.

Protect the patient from heat loss or gain—use a log roll onto insulation.

Monitor and treat for shock (see page 104).

Repeat check for injuries.

Send for evacuation help as soon as feasible.

Chest Injuries
Penetrating Wound of the Chest

Chest injuries cause one out of four deaths from trauma in the United States. A chest injury in the mountains is a particular cause for concern. Any penetrating injury to the chest is potentially serious. A penetrating injury to the chest can result from a fall onto a sharp object, such as a rock or an ice ax.

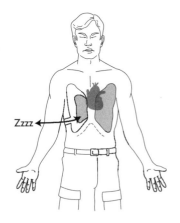

A penetrating injury can cause a collapsed lung and death from a lack of oxygen. In normal respiration, the chest expands and air is drawn in through the mouth and nose. When the chest relaxes, air is pushed out. A hole in the chest wall creates another route for the air to go in and out, causing a "sucking sound" on both inhalation and exhalation. Air can be trapped between the lung and chest wall, putting pressure on the lung itself. When part or all of a lung collapses under this pressure, the patient experiences increasing difficulty in breathing.

First Aid Goals. The goals of first aid for a penetrating wound to the chest are to assess the seriousness of the injury, prevent further injury, help increase the ease of breathing, and watch closely for changes.

Assess Seriousness. It is important to assess the seriousness of the wound as soon as possible. A serious wound to the chest can kill someone just about as quickly as a severed artery. When a chest injury is suspected, bare the chest in order to look and listen. If you need to turn the patient over to see and treat the wound, then you must stabilize embedded objects and protect the neck as the patient is rolled.

Prevent Further Injury. In order to keep the patient's condition from worsening, follow these steps:

1. Seal the hole as quickly as possible, with your bare hand if necessary.
2. Cover the wound with a sterile dressing several times larger than the hole itself in order to avoid it being sucked into the hole.
3. Cover the dressing with a piece of occlusive material slightly larger than the dressing, such as a piece of plastic wrap or aluminum foil, to block the flow of air.

4. Tape the dressing in place on all sides except for one corner. This allows air to escape during exhalation but prevents it from entering during inhalation.
5. Stabilize any embedded object, if necessary.

Help Increase the Ease of Breathing. Place the patient in a position that is most comfortable and results in the greatest ease of breathing.

Watch Closely for Changes. Observe the patient at regular intervals for any changes in breathing. If the patient experiences increased difficulty in breathing, the occlusive dressing must be checked to make sure air is not being trapped inside the chest and exerting pressure on the lungs and heart. Lift the seal briefly. If trapped air escapes and the patient feels immediate relief, then the seal may need to be vented at intervals. Use the patient's condition as your guide. Immediate evacuation should be undertaken.

FIRST AID FOR PENETRATING WOUND OF THE CHEST

1. Seal the wound.
2. Cover with a sterile dressing.
3. Cover the dressing with an occlusive dressing or bandage.
4. Tape in place, leaving one corner untaped.
5. Help the patient to a position that is most comfortable for breathing.
6. Watch closely for changes.
7. Evacuate the patient as quickly as possible.

Rib Fractures

Most rib fractures, breaks in the bones, are caused by falls. The major symptom of rib fracture is pain, localized over the injured area, which worsens with deep breathing. Signs are deformity and bruising, but these may be subtle or absent. Rib fractures vary in severity from a simple single broken rib to multiple ribs broken in several places.

First Aid Goals. The goals of first aid for rib fractures are to assess the seriousness of the injury, help increase the ease of breathing, and watch closely for changes.

Assess Seriousness. Get down to bare skin to determine the number of ribs involved. Put a dressing on any open wound you find. Observe how deeply (or shallowly) the patient is breathing.

Help Increase the Ease of Breathing. When there are one or two broken ribs, an improvised pillow, such as a rolled sweater, can be placed over the injured area for comfort. The patient can hold it in place, if desired. The padding may be loosely taped in place, as long as the taping does NOT restrict breathing.

If several ribs are fractured in multiple places, a section of ribs may become loose and move independently of the rest of the chest. The section will usually move in the opposite direction of the rest of the chest wall. This condition, flail chest, is life threatening, and the patient needs immediate evacuation. Position the patient to help ease breathing: sitting is likely to be the most comfortable position. Some patients may not be able to sit. In that case, place the patient with the injured side down. The patient may feel more comfortable if a pillow or other padding is placed against the section of ribs. **Do nothing** that restricts the patient's efforts to breathe.

FIRST AID FOR RIB FRACTURES

Identify the area of the injury.
Support the injured area with a pillow or article of clothing.
Help the patient to a position that is most comfortable for breathing.
DO NOTHING THAT RESTRICTS EFFORTS TO BREATHE.
Watch the patient for changes in breathing.
Evacuate as soon as possible.

Watch Closely for Changes. Watch for any change in breathing. The patient should be encouraged to breathe as deeply as possible to avoid the possibility of developing pneumonia. Evacuate the patient as soon as possible.

Other Chest Injuries: Pneumothorax (Collapsed Lung)

Life-threatening damage to the lungs can occur without penetrating wounds or rib fractures. The lungs may be torn by trauma or in some instances spontaneously develop small tears where the lung touches the chest wall. Air escapes through these tears into the chest and begins to put pressure on the lungs, heart, and major blood vessels. The patient will develop difficulty breathing and pain on respiration. The veins in the neck may be distended. Signs and symptoms of shock (see page 104) may develop. Immediate evacuation and medical treatment are necessary. A patient may be able to walk out with assistance if not required to carry a pack or other gear.

Prevention of Chest Injuries

Chest injury can be related to the improper use of ice axes and ropes. Guards over the sharp pick, adz, and spike of an ice ax can prevent injury. Individual guards can be removed one at a time as conditions warrant. The adz cover, for example, rarely needs to be removed except when chopping steps in hard snow or ice.

Abdominal Injuries

Open abdominal wounds may be obvious, particularly when there are protruding intestines. Do not attempt to replace these organs into the abdomen. Cover the wound and any protruding organs with a sterile dressing or dressings. These dressings may be moistened with sterile water (see page 69). Then place an occlusive bandage, such as a piece of plastic wrap, over the sterile dressing to prevent drying out of the abdominal contents. Tape down the edges of the occlusive barrier. Place an article of clothing over the bandage to help the patient remain warm. The patient may be more comfortable positioned lying with the knees bent to decrease pressure on the abdomen. Evacuate the patient as soon as possible.

A closed injury to the abdomen is less obvious, and thus may be more dangerous, since it can delay recognition of a life-threatening injury. The mechanism of injury, such as a significant fall landing on the chest and abdomen or a long tumble down a snowfield, should suggest internal abdominal injury. The signs and symptoms of internal injury may only be those of shock (see page 104). Signs such as bruising and abdominal rigidity or tenderness may be found. The patient may also have a gradually increasing pulse rate, appear pale, and feel nauseated. First aid in the mountains is limited to close observation of the patient, treatment for shock, and evacuation as soon as possible. A careful written record of the signs and symptoms you observe may be very useful to the surgeon in the hospital.

Extremity Injuries

Fractures, Dislocations, Sprains, and Strains

Bones come together at joints, which in turn are held together by ligaments. A break or crack in a bone is called a *fracture*. When a bone end is displaced from a joint, it is called a *dislocation*. When a joint is bent beyond its limits and a ligament or any other soft tissue around a joint is torn, it is called a *sprain*. A *strain,* on the other hand, is an overstretched muscle.

Like wounds, fractures are classified as either closed or open, depending on whether the skin is broken. An open fracture can result from either a direct blow or an indirect force, such as a twisting injury, causing the broken bone end to push through the skin.

Fractures can be recognized by symptoms and signs. The patient will report pain, a reluctance to use the extremity, and possibly may have heard or felt a snap or crack. The examiner may find deformity (compare to the uninjured side), tenderness around the full circumference of the limb or at one specific point on the limb, swelling, instability, or bruising (later), and possibly may hear a grating sound as the broken bone ends rub against each other. Because blood vessels and nerves travel alongside the bone, jagged bone ends can cause serious damage. First aid for fractures is splinting.

Dislocations occur at joints, most commonly at the shoulder or hip. The patient will report pain and a loss of the ability to use the joint. The examiner may find deformity, shortening of a limb compared to the uninjured limb, tenderness, or occasionally swelling. The joint may seem "locked" in position. The displaced bone end may cut off circulation or impinge on nerves. First aid for dislocations is splinting.

Sprains also occur at joints, most commonly at the ankle or knee. The patient will report pain, aggravated by motion. The examiner will find localized tenderness and swelling. First aid for sprains is rest, ice, compression, elevation, and stabilization (RICES), discussed in a following section.

Strains occur when a muscle has been overstretched by exercise, by lifting something too heavy, or by a sudden or uncoordinated movement. The patient will report pain or a burning feeling. The examiner will find localized tenderness and swelling generally in areas between joints. Strains are commonly found in the neck, back, thighs, or lower legs. First aid for strains is RICES.

It can be difficult, especially in the mountaineering setting, to tell precisely whether an injury is a fracture, a dislocation, or a sprain. It is even difficult at times for doctors in a hospital to tell, which is why they have X-ray machines. Dislocations often have associated fractures. So, if you have any doubt, **always treat an extremity injury as if a fracture were present.**

EXTREMITY INJURIES

SIGNS AND SYMPTOMS	FIRST AID
Fracture—Break in a bone	
Pain	Splinting
Reluctance to use the extremity	
Heard or felt a snap, crack, or grating sound	
Deformity (compared to the uninjured side)	
Tenderness	
Swelling	
Bruising	
Dislocation—Displacement of a bone from a joint	
Pain	Splinting
Loss of ability to move the joint	
Deformity or shortening	
Tenderness	
Swelling	
Sprains—Tear of ligament or soft tissue around a joint	
Pain, aggravated by motion	RICES
Tenderness	
Swelling	
Strain—Overstretched muscle	
Tenderness	RICES
Swelling	

First Aid Goals. The first aid goals for extremity injuries are to assess the seriousness of the injury, prevent further injury by reducing movement, and control pain.

Assess Seriousness. Breathing and circulation take priority. It is easy to become so involved with a gruesome extremity injury that the needs of the total patient are neglected. A fracture can wait. The airway cannot.

Assess the patient for the signs and symptoms of shock (see page 104). A fracture of the pelvis or femur (upper leg) often results in shock because of serious internal bleeding. These injuries are potentially life threatening.

Assessment of the seriousness of the injury requires baring the skin for a good look at the extremity. You may have to remove several layers, cut some clothes, or remove a boot. You may miss an open fracture if you do not get down to bare skin. A serious complication of an extremity injury can result from the fact that blood vessels and nerves travel alongside the bone and may be injured by jagged bone ends. Thus, *examination of the patient must include a check for a pulse beyond the site of the injury toward the affected hand or foot.* When the injury has affected the blood flow, evacuation must be as soon as possible. The best indicator of adequate blood flow is the presence of a pulse below the site of the injury. Pulses are sometimes difficult to find, even on uninjured limbs. When a pulse cannot be found, a check for capillary refill may be used to ascertain circulation.

Prevent Further Injury. The basic principle for preventing further injury is immobilization. This can range from the temporary immobilization for a suspected sprained joint to rigid immobilization for a suspected fracture.

Using RICES on a suspected sprain of the ankle or knee may allow the patient to walk out, but the potential exists for making the injury worse. A suspected sprain may actually be a fracture. In general, let pain be your guide. If the injury is too painful to walk on, then don't. You may need to wait 1 to 1½ hours before making the decision about walking out, but there is no advantage to getting a short distance down the trail to a place where you don't want to be and then not being able to go any farther.

Rest, Ice, Compression, Elevation, and Stabilization (RICES)

First aid for sprains and strains consists of a sequence of five steps, designed to reduce the damage and the swelling. RICES is also used to reduce swelling and pain in fractures. The last step, Stabilization, may be necessary or possible for some strains, such as a strain of the lower back.

- *Rest.* After an injury has occurred, stop. Continuing to use an injured arm or leg can result in extending the amount of damage done. Walking on a badly twisted knee or ankle can result in further damage and lead to a much prolonged recovery time. After an injury, stop and give the extremity a chance to rest.

- *Ice.* A stuff sack filled with snow or a chemical ice pack should be placed on the injured area. The application of cold will reduce the development of swelling and speed recovery. To prevent frostbite, place a layer of cloth between the cold pack and the skin. Keep the ice in place for 20 minutes and then remove it for at least 10 minutes. The cold pack should be applied at least three or four times a day and may be continued for three days after the injury. Apply a compression bandage after a period of icing.

- *Compression.* Compression provided by an elastic wrap can further reduce the development of swelling. The wrap should be comfortably tight. Check below the level of the injury for a pulse to ensure that the elastic wrap has not been too tightly applied. If circulation is compromised, or the patient experiences pain, tingling, or numbness, the wrap is too tight and must be loosened.

- *Elevation.* Swelling will be further limited if the injured part is elevated to a position slightly above the level of the heart.
- *Stabilization.* Splint the injured part to prevent additional injury.

After the first few hours of RICES, the injury can be reevaluated for seriousness. If the signs and symptoms indicate that the injury is limited to a sprain or strain, the patient may try to use the part. Effort should be made to use as natural motions as possible when using the injured part. Walking with a limp can place much greater stress on the joint. Using a natural motion puts the least amount of load on the injured area. The patient should carry as little weight as possible. If severe pain remains or if pain increases, the part should again receive the RICES treatment and further use should be delayed until another day.

Splinting

General Principles of Splinting. Having an organized approach to splinting is essential. Don't just do something, stand there and figure out what you are going to do.

1. *Determine the location and extent of the injury* by looking and feeling. Get down to skin. Begin above the injury site (a point close to the body) and move to below the injury site (toward the hand or foot) to determine the extent of the injury. Check for circulation below the injury, and assess sensation and movement below the injury (fingers or toes).
2. If there is an open fracture, *stop the bleeding* with direct pressure. Put a dressing on all open wounds before applying a splint. The wound site must be accessible even after the splint has been tied.
3. If there are exposed bone ends covered with dirt and debris, the *dirt should be rinsed off* with large amounts of water. Use water that has been previously purified by boiling or chemical treatment to reduce the likelihood of infection.
4. *If the extremity is severely bent out of its normal shape* (angulated) and IF the injury is *not at a joint,* **then** firmly but gently straighten the limb. When the limb is severely angulated, it may be difficult to apply a splint. In addition, a severely angulated injury can cut off circulation. The advice "splint them where they lie" means that the patient is not to be moved before the splint has been applied. The limb occasionally must be moved to restore normal position, especially when there is a badly distorted break. A steady, firm but gentle pull in the direction of the long axis of the extremity is applied while the portion of the extremity above the fracture is supported by another person.

   IF the injury is at a joint (for example, the elbow or the knee) and if there is no pulse below (and the hand or foot is cold and discolored), **then** *pull gently to straighten* it until a pulse returns. The limb should *not* be straightened when there is a suspected dislocation and the circulation below the joint is good.

5. Gently remove rings, watches, boots, or any other item of jewelry or clothing that could cause constriction of the area once swelling has occurred (swelling **will** occur).

6. *Prepare a splint* that is of appropriate material, the right size, and padded. Splints, which can be either improvised or commercial, can also be either rigid or soft. Rigid splints can be improvised from a pack-frame stay, an ice ax, tent poles, a spare ski tip, or tightly rolled closed cell foam. A makeshift sling can be improvised by using safety pins to pin a sleeve to the front of the jacket. Tree branches are overrated as sources for splints, as they are difficult to remove from trees if they are still attached, are generally brittle and easily broken if they are not still attached to the tree, and are non-existent above timberline. Many mountaineers carry a metal splint in order to avoid tying up some other object (such as an ice ax) that may have another important use. Soft splints include blankets, extra clothing, slings, or any soft material that can be used to immobilize a broken bone. When there is absolutely nothing available for improvising a splint or when there may not be enough time to construct a splint, as in an emergency rescue situation, you can always use another body part as an anatomic splint. Tie an injured extremity to an uninjured part of the body. Tie a broken leg to a good leg, for example, or bind an arm to the chest.

The basic rule of immobilization of an extremity injury is to immobilize both adjacent joints. Thus, if the forearm is injured, immobilize the wrist and the elbow (and the forearm between). If the lower leg is injured, immobilize the ankle and the knee. A rigid splint of the correct size must be long enough to immobilize the joint above and the joint below the injury, or a combination of splint and ties must be able to immobilize both joints. Measure the uninjured extremity to estimate the proper size.

The final step in preparing the splint is making sure that it is adequately padded. Be certain to fill hollows, such as inside the palm of the hand or at the ankle or knee. A splint must support an injured extremity evenly throughout its entire length, exerting equal pressure on both protrusions and hollows, so that the limb will not move inside the splint.

Do not overpad the splint. Unnecessary padding will make it

difficult to secure the splint to the limb and provide adequate support to the fracture.

7. Tie the splint on gently but firmly: too loose and the splint will not immobilize the break; too tight and you will create a tourniquet. The ties should be just above and below the fracture, as well as at the adjacent joints. Tie the knots in an accessible place.

8. Neatness counts. A hastily made knot may come undone, a wrinkle in padding can cause the patient pain, and a rumpled sling will loosen and allow a broken forearm to move out of position. Put in one knot only per tie and cut off long ends. Multiple knots in a tie will make it difficult to disassemble a splint if necessary to improve circulation or comfort.

9. Observe areas below the injury site for circulation and sensation, and repeat this observation at least every half hour. If the patient complains of numbness or tingling in the fingers or toes or is unable to straighten them, or if there is any indication of decreased circulation, then check the tightness of the ties immediately. Swelling may have made your "just right" ties too tight, and they may have to be loosened. Fingertips and toes need to be accessible for these observations.

10. When possible, elevate the injured extremity. Elevation can slow the development of swelling and reduce pain. If the patient is warm, cold compresses can be applied to the injury site to reduce pain and delay swelling.

BASIC PRINCIPLES OF SPLINTING

1. Determine the location and extent of the injury and check for circulation below the injury.
2. Stop bleeding, where necessary.
3. Rinse dirt off exposed bone ends, cover with sterile dressing.
4. Straighten badly angulated limbs by gentle pulling.
5. Remove any jewelry or clothing that will later cause constriction of the limb.
6. Prepare a splint, size it, and pad it.
7. Tie the splint on.
8. Neatness counts.
9. Observe below the site for circulation and sensation.
10. Elevate the injured extremity. Apply cold compresses to the injury site.

Specific Procedures for Immobilization. These specific instructions for splinting use the principles explained above. Be sure to observe all principles of splinting, including checks for circulation and sensation.

Mid-Shaft Fracture of the Upper Arm: *soft and anatomic splint.* The fractured bone is supported against the padded chest wall, the sling prevents downward motion from the forearm, and the swathe prevents motion of the elbow away from the body.

1. Prepare materials: a dressing of appropriate size if a wound is present, padding material to place between the broken arm and the chest wall, two triangular bandages, safety pins.
2. Have the patient support the lower arm with the unaffected hand.
3. Place and secure a dressing on the wound (if necessary).
4. Place padding between the broken arm and the chest wall.
5. Fold a triangular bandage so that it will make an 8-inch-wide sling to support the wrist and mid-shaft of the lower arm.
6. Place one end of the triangular bandage next to the neck on the uninjured side, and let the second end fall in front of the chest and between the broken arm and body.
7. Bring the second end of the triangular bandage up and around the neck, and adjust the sling so that the wrist is supported by the sling. The hand should be level with the elbow and the fingers should be visible.
8. Fasten the two ends on the side of the neck.
9. Fold the second triangular bandage to make a 5- to 6-inch-wide swathe.
10. Place the swathe over the lower portion of the upper arm on the injured side to secure the arm to the chest wall. Fasten the swathe in front on the unaffected side.
11. Secure the padding to the patient's clothing or the swathe with safety pins.
12. Check the pulse at the wrist, and check for capillary refill in the fingers. Adjust the splint as necessary.

Fracture of the Elbow: *padded ladder splint and sling.* The padded metal splint stabilizes the broken elbow, while the sling supports the arm in place.

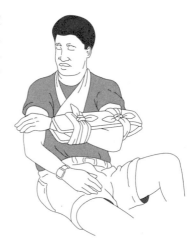

1. Prepare materials: a flexible aluminum-foam splint, Sam Splint, or a ladder splint; padding for the splint; roller bandages to secure the splint; and a triangular bandage. Bend the ladder into an elongated U shape. The bottom of the U should be only as wide as the breadth of the arm.
2. Do not move the arm. Splint it in the position found.
3. Position the padded splint on either side of the arm. The elbow forms one angle of a triangle, the other two angles are formed where the splint crosses the arm.
4. Secure the splint to the upper arm and forearm with soft roller bandages.
5. Fold a triangular bandage so that it will make a 3-inch-wide sling to support the weight of the arm.
6. Place one end of the sling next to the neck on the uninjured side, and let the second end fall in front of the chest and between the broken arm and body.
7. Bring the second end of the triangular bandage up and around the neck, and adjust the sling so that the wrist is supported by the sling. The hand should be above the elbow and the fingers should be visible.
8. Fasten the two ends on the side of the neck.
9. Check the pulse at the wrist, and check for capillary refill in the fingers.

Fracture of the Forearm: *rigid splint with sling and swathe.* The sling supports the arm in place, and is useful for fractures of both the collarbone and the arm, but does not by itself immobilize either the elbow joint or the shoulder joint. The swathe binds the arm in place to the body.

1. Prepare materials: rigid material the length of the forearm, padding materials, ties, and two triangular bandages.

2. Place the padded rigid splint under the wrist and arm. Place padding in the palm of the hand.
3. Using roller gauze or cravats, tie the splint to the arm at the wrist and elbow. The tie at the wrist will cover the lower portion of the hand, including the thumb.

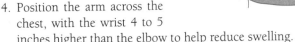
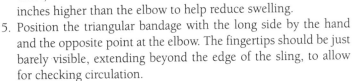

4 OR 5 INCHES

4. Position the arm across the chest, with the wrist 4 to 5 inches higher than the elbow to help reduce swelling.
5. Position the triangular bandage with the long side by the hand and the opposite point at the elbow. The fingertips should be just barely visible, extending beyond the edge of the sling, to allow for checking circulation.
6. Tie a knot at the side of the neck, and place a pad underneath.
7. Pin or tie the elbow end to form a pocket for the elbow.
8. Place the swathe across the chest, horizontally. It should be fairly wide where it goes over the injured arm. The swathe prevents motion of the arm away from the body.
9. Check the pulse at the wrist, and check for capillary refill in the fingers.

Fracture of the Pelvis: Any fracture of the bones forming the hips (pelvis) is potentially life threatening due to significant blood loss into body cavities. Fractures are associated with direct heavy forces that crush the pelvis or indirect forces transmitted to the pelvis; for example, when a knee is slammed into a rock and the femur is forcefully pushed against the pelvis. Open fractures are unusual, and blood loss will usually be detected through signs and symptoms of shock (see page 104). Pelvic fractures are suspected when the mechanism of injury suggests a fracture and there are signs of tenderness or grating sounds when the pelvis is examined. There is no specific splint to be applied in the field. The patient will need to be evacuated on a rigid stretcher as soon as possible. While waiting for evacuation, make the patient as comfortable as possible and treat for shock.

Fracture of the Femur: splinting an *upper leg injury*. A fracture of the upper leg (femur) can be a very painful and serious injury. The ends of the broken bones may be pulled out of alignment by the strong muscles of the upper leg. This can cause further pain and damage, with blood pooling inside the muscles. In contrast, some femur fractures will not be misaligned and pain is limited. Traction splints help stabilize the broken bones in fractures where the bones have become misaligned. By putting traction on the leg (by pulling on the foot), the bone ends may be moved to a more normal position and spasm of the thigh muscles is reduced.

Traction splints are difficult to improvise with climbing or hiking equipment, although an acceptable splint can be constructed of tall cross-country ski poles and a number of strong triangular bandages. The top of the splint, to be placed under the injured leg near the buttocks, is formed by interlocking the hand loops of the poles. The top of the splint can be further secured by tying the ski pole tops together, across the top of the leg, with a strong cravat. This cravat should hold the poles in place on opposite sides of the leg without being tightly tied. The baskets of the poles are tied together and form the bottom of the splint. Two triangular bandages are folded into 5- or 6-inch-wide cravats. One is looped around the ankle as a hitch, and the second is used to connect the hitch to the bottom of the poles. Traction is developed by twisting the lower cravat like a windlass. Serious damage can be done to the patient's ankle and foot if the traction either cuts off circulation or presses on nerves. Special training is required to use either an improvised or commercial splint and is beyond the scope of this book.

At a minimum, the patient's legs should be tied together, with padding placed between the legs. The patient's legs could be supported by the use of a ladderlike frame from an external-frame backpack placed under the legs. A fracture of the femur near the knee should be supported by the use of a splint placed on the back of the leg. The patient will need to be transported on a rigid stretcher. A fracture of the upper leg, even if it is only suspected, should be a cause for prompt evacuation.

Fracture of the Knee: *padded aluminum-foam splint.* The splint described for use with a broken elbow may be adapted for use with a knee. Use this splint when the knee is found in a bent position. If the patient is in a sitting position, back support will be needed. Alternatively, the patient may be more comfortable in a lying position.

1. Prepare materials: a Sam Splint, padding for the splint, roller bandages to secure the splint, and stuff bags or small packs filled with clothing to support the knee and leg. Bend the ladder into

an elongated U shape. The bottom of the U should be only as wide as the breadth of the lower leg.

2. Do not move the knee or leg. Splint it in the position found.

3. Position the padded splint on either side of the lower and upper leg, with the open end of the splint on either side of the upper leg. The knee forms one angle of a triangle, the other two angles are formed where the splint crosses the upper and lower leg.

4. Secure the ladder splint to the upper and lower leg with soft roller bandages.

5. Place sufficient padding between the knee and the ground to support the leg.

6. Check the pulse below the splint at the ankle or foot, and check for capillary refill in the toes.

If the patient's leg is found flat with the knee unbent, splint the leg in the unbent position using a long rigid splint with sufficient padding to ensure comfort. Alternatively, a ladderlike frame from an external-frame backpack could be placed under both knees, with the long axis of the frame parallel to the legs. Place padding between the legs and the frame, and secure the splint with ties. The patient will need to be transported by stretcher.

Mid-Shaft Fracture of the Lower Leg: *rigid splint* for a lower leg injury.
1. Prepare materials: rigid splint that extends from above the knee to the ankle, padding for the splint, dressing of appropriate size if a wound is present, padding material to place between the legs, four cravats.
2. Check the pulse in the foot. While one first aider supports the leg from above the ankle, a second first aider removes the boot or shoe. It is critical to have access to the toes to check circulation. A boot on the foot is necessary only if the patient intends to walk on it. A down bootie and/or several pairs of socks can be used for protection. It is possible to cut an inspection hole in the tip of the socks and then cover the toes with another sock. In this way only one sock needs to be removed to check circulation.
3. Support the foot and leg. A first aider grasps the ankle and exerts a gentle, steady pull on the leg to stabilize the foot. Maintain the pressure until the splint has been completely tied on.
4. Place and secure a dressing on the wound if necessary.
5. Place four 2-inch-wide cravats underneath the broken leg, using the space under the knee or ankle for access to place the cravats. Cravats are placed at the knee, the ankle, and 2 inches above and below the break.
6. Place the padded rigid splint next to the outer side of the fractured leg (not between legs). Add padding to fill in spaces between the rigid splint and the leg.
7. Secure the splint with the two cravats to either side of the fracture. Tie the knots over the splint. Tie the cravats at the knee and the ankle.
8. Adjust the cravats so that the splint is snug but not tight.
9. If using an ice ax, the adz end should be at the foot with the adz at the heel and the pick at the toes. The ball of the foot may be tied to the pick to support the foot at a right angle to the leg.
10. Have the patient flex his or her toes toward the head. If the patient is unable to move his or her toes or the movement causes severe pain, then the cravats are tied too tightly.
11. Check the pulse at the ankle or check for capillary refill in the toes. Adjust cravats as needed. Additional cravats may be used to tie the legs together.

Ankle Fracture: *"pillow" splint*. This soft splint allows protection of the injured area with a maximum of comfort.
1. Prepare materials: blanket or bulky jacket, three cravats or triangular bandages.

2. Gently remove the shoe or boot. One first aider supports the ankle from above the injury while a second first aider removes the shoe.
3. Wrap a bulky jacket or vest around the foot and ankle.
4. Tie it in place with at least three ties. Safety pins make an acceptable substitute if cravats are unavailable.

Burns

Burns can be classified according to the depth of damage to the skin. A *superficial burn* involves only the top layer of skin. There is reddening of the skin, mild pain, and slight swelling. The average sunburn is a typical superficial burn. A *partial-thickness burn* involves the top layers of the skin. There is blistering of the skin, mild to moderate pain, and moderate swelling over a period of days. A *full-thickness burn* involves damage to all layers of the skin and to underlying tissues; it may appear white or charred and causes moderate to severe pain. Pain may be absent in the full-thickness burn if nerve endings have been killed by the burn, although less severely burned tissue surrounding the full-thickness burn may be very painful.

Some burns are critical, life threatening, or may cause permanent disfigurement and require advanced medical care. The severity of a burn is also related to its location and extent, as well as the patient's age.

CRITICAL AND LIFE-THREATENING BURNS

Burns causing difficulty in breathing or damage to the mouth or nose

Partial-thickness burns covering more than 15 percent of the body or more than one body part

Full-thickness burns covering 5 percent or more of the body

Burns to head, neck, hands, feet, or genitals

Burns caused by chemicals, explosions, electricity, or lightning

Any partial- or full-thickness burn to a child or elderly person

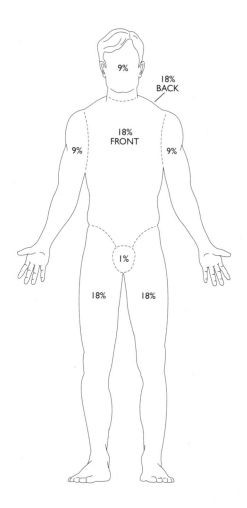

A guide to estimating the body surface involved is the rule of nines. In an adult, the head and each of the arms equals 9 percent of the body surface. Each leg equals 18 percent, as does the front of the trunk and the back of the trunk. A burn to the back (18 percent) and one arm (9 percent) would cover 27 percent of the body surface.

First Aid Goals. The priorities in burn care are to prevent further injury or contamination of the wound, relieve pain, and assess and treat other injuries.

Prevention of Further Injury. First, **cool off the heat!** Pour cool water on the burned area or immerse it in water immediately, unless the affected area is already cool. There may still be enough heat retained in the burned tissues, or in smoldering clothing, to increase the damage. Remove all burned clothing. Removing the heat should be a priority in protecting the patient from further harm and be done in **Step 4** of first aid response. Once the heat has been removed, additional care may proceed at a slower pace and be accomplished during Step 7. Small fragments of adhered cloth should not be removed from the burn wound. Don't break blisters because an open wound is more likely to become infected.

Treatment of Thermal Burns

Minor Burns: If the burn is superficial or partial thickness with unbroken blisters, the burned area can be immersed in cold water to relieve the pain. The part can remain immersed for 30 minutes, or until the pain subsides. Afterwards, protect blisters by covering with a dry sterile dressing.

  Major Burns: If the burn is partial thickness with broken blisters or is suspected to be full thickness, then the burn care is as follows:

1. Cool the burn immediately.
2. Carefully wash the burned area with a sterile gauze pad, soap, and sterile water.
3. Remove all rings or other tight jewelry from the affected area.
4. Spread a thin layer of antibiotic ointment over the wound if medical care is to be delayed more than a few hours.
5. Apply a dry, sterile dressing.
6. Pain can be relieved by wrapping the burned area with additional layers of dressing to exclude air. Ice packs or chemical cold packs may also be used, over the dressings, for pain relief. Avoid overcooling the patient or freezing burnt tissue.
7. Elevate a burned extremity.
8. Assess the patient thoroughly. Be aware that fractures are commonly found along with major burns. Similarly, head and facial burns require especially thorough physical examination and monitoring.
9. Look for signs and symptoms of shock (see page 104) and treat if necessary. Provide the patient with as much water as he or she can drink. Help the patient maintain adequate body temperature.
10. Any patient with a critical burn or a suspected full-thickness burn over 5 percent of the body surface area or a partial-thickness burn of over 15 percent should be evacuated as soon as possible.

FIRST AID FOR MAJOR BURNS

1. Cool the burn immediately; flush or brush off chemical agents.
2. Wash the burned area.
3. Remove rings.
4. Spread a thin layer of antibiotic ointment.
5. Apply a dry, sterile dressing.
6. Wrap with more layers to occlude air.
7. Elevate a burned extremity.
8. Assess the patient thoroughly.
9. Treat for shock as needed.
10. Evacuate as indicated.

When evacuation is not indicated, or is not possible, change the dressing every day, as with any other wound. If the dressing adheres to the wound, soak it with sterile water (see page 69) for a few minutes. Removal should then be easy. Nonadherent dressings are particularly useful. Look for signs of infection.

Treatment of Chemical Burns. Liquid chemicals causing a burn must be immediately flushed from the skin with large amounts of cool water. Brush dry chemicals off with a cloth or gloved hand first. Water may be used to flush off any residue remaining on the skin. Removing the chemical must be done during **Step 4** of first aid response to ensure that further damage is prevented. Make sure that the chemical is not flushed onto other parts of the body. If only one eye has been affected, flush the burned eye from the nose outward to avoid washing the chemical into the unaffected eye. After all traces of the chemical have been removed, additional treatment may proceed at a slower pace during Step 7. Treat the burn as a thermal burn, and evacuate the patient.

Treatment of Lightning Burns. A thorough physical examination is necessary in the case of a patient of lightning injury because the electrical current may have passed through the body. These burns usually will have an entrance as well as an exit wound. Although the skin may not appear to be extensively damaged, severe damage to internal tissues may have occurred. Other lightning burns may be limited to the skin because the current "flashed over" the skin's surface and did not enter the body. Do not cool lightning or other electrical burns with water.

The patient may be found unconscious and in respiratory and cardiac arrest. Prolonged CPR may be needed but has a high rate of success. Treat wounds as any burn or open wound. Fractures of the limbs is common and must be treated. The patient should be evacuated as soon as possible as lightning injuries are potentially severe (see page 44 for CPR and page 145 for additional information about lightning injuries).

Prevention. The worst burns in mountaineering occur when a tent catches fire with someone inside. Cook outside of tents whenever possible, and always position stoves so that escape is easy if an unexpected fire begins. Most tents sold today use flame-retardant materials, but not all do. Special care should be taken in the handling of stoves and fuels.

Sunburn and Snowblindness

Sunburn
The most frequent burns in the mountains are sunburns. The atmosphere, which screens out most of the harmful ultraviolet (UV) rays, is thinner at higher altitudes, and thus mountaineers are at greater risk of sunburn. Travel across snowfields or glaciers can be a source of particularly severe sunburns on a sunny day. A bad burn can occur on even a cloudy day. Reflected light can burn the inside of your mouth or the underside of your nose. Prevention of sunburn is important because it is associated with an increased risk of skin cancer.

First Aid Goals. The first aid goals are to prevent further injury, prevent contamination of open blisters, and reduce pain.

Prevent Further Injury. Sunburned skin should be covered with opaque clothing to prevent additional damage, or the patient should end exposure to the sun.

Treatment. Sunburn should be treated like any other burn.

Prevention. Prevention is more effective than any first aid. For the first outing of the season, an exposure of more than 15 minutes without protection should be avoided. Later in the season, after tanning, the exposure time may be lengthened. Opaque hats, scarves, or handkerchiefs worn about the head also provide protection from sunburn. No matter how bizarre the effect, the use of hats and scarves can be very worthwhile. Many lightweight clothes provide very little protection from the sun. Individuals who burn easily may want to ensure that clothing is opaque to the sun or purchase clothing that is rated to provide protection.

Additionally, you can use protective creams or ointments. These come in two types: opaque or physical agents, such as zinc oxide or clown white; and chemical sunscreen agents. Because individuals vary widely in their tolerance to sun exposure (from fair-haired, light-skinned, easily burned to dark-haired, dark-skinned, easily tanned), sunscreens come in different ratings. The sunscreen protection factor (SPF) is based on the amount of time necessary to produce minimal reddening or sunburn from sun exposure. An SPF of 15 indicates that when the sunscreen is used it takes 15 times the amount of exposure to produce sunburn than when the sunscreen is not used. Another characteristic of sunscreens is how well they stay on the body. A sunscreen should be water resistant, as sweating is common (and persistent) in mountaineering settings. Choose a preparation that has the highest SPF rating and will not dissolve in perspiration or rub off easily.

PREVENTING SUNBURN

Limit first sun exposure of the season to 15 minutes.
Build up a tan slowly.
Wear opaque clothes or clothes treated to limit exposure to UV light.
Use a water-resistant chemical sunblock with a high SPF, and reapply frequently.

Snowblindness

Snowblindness is not "blindness" at all, but rather sunburn of the surface of the eye. The surface of the eye is more sensitive to UV radiation than the skin, and travel on snow or any bright, reflective surface can cause injury to the eyes if they are not properly protected. Just as in a skin sunburn, the injury does not become obvious until several hours after the exposure. Snowblindness usually resolves in time, but permanent damage to the retina has been reported. Repeated bouts of snowblindness may be related to development of cataracts later in life.

Snowblindness is recognized more by the patient's symptoms than by objective physical signs. All that is visible to the observer are eyes that are bloodshot and tearing. The patient may initially complain of eyes that feel simply irritated or dry. Some patients mistakenly believe that there is an object in the eye. Severe symptoms include feeling as if the eyes are "full of sand" and pain when moving or blinking the eyes.

First Aid Goals. The first aid goals are to prevent further injury to the eyes and reduce pain.

Prevent Further Injury. If symptoms are minor, protect the eyes from further exposure to the sun. Dark goggles or sunglasses with side shields are useful. Using both together is best for someone with initial symptoms of snowblindness. The protection of a single pair of sunglasses can be improved by placing tape over the lenses, leaving a horizontal slit to see through. Side shields can also be improvised, as can a "Lone Ranger"-style mask with narrow slits, made from cardboard or similar material. Rubbing the eyes can cause further damage. Pain can be relieved by cool wet compresses.

Treatment. If symptoms are severe, contact lenses must be removed (see page 58). Patch the eyes firmly for at least 12 hours and have the patient rest. If pain has not resolved, patches may be replaced for another 12 hours. Aspirin or ibuprofen can be helpful for pain.

Prevention. To prevent snowblindness, be sure to buy sunglasses that are rated to prevent transmission of the greatest amount of UVB and UVA radiation (preferably 90 percent, for mountaineering use) and have side shields. It is also a good idea to carry an emergency pair of collapsible dark glasses made of coated plastic that prevents the transmission of UVB and UVA light.

SNOWBLINDNESS

SIGNS AND SYMPTOMS	FIRST AID
Eye appears bloodshot and teary	Remove contacts
Eye initially feels dry or irritated	Patch eyes for at least 12 hours
Later, eye feels "full of sand" and painful when blinking	Rest
	Give aspirin or ibuprofen for pain

PREVENTION
Wear sunglasses rated to stop transmission of UVA and UVB. Wear side shields. At high altitudes, wear sunglasses on overcast days as well as sunny.

SHOCK

Shock is a process resulting from collapse of the cardiovascular system. This system distributes oxygen and other nutrients to all portions of the body as well as transports carbon dioxide and other waste products from the cells. The cardiovascular system has three major components: the heart, which acts as a pump; the blood, which is pumped through the system and carries the oxygen and other nutrients and removes carbon dioxide and other waste products; and the arteries and veins, which act as the "pipes" through which the blood flows. The blood vessels are more than simple static pipes. The veins have valves to prevent the backflow of blood in the wrong direction. Arteries are surrounded by muscles that help maintain the pressure needed to ensure circulation of the blood. Damage to any of these components can result in shock. If the heart weakens, stops pumping, or beats irregularly, *cardiogenic shock* occurs. If blood is lost through internal or external bleeding, *hemorrhagic shock* occurs. If blood volume is decreased by severe dehydration, heat-related illness, or a long bout of vomiting or diarrhea, **metabolic shock** occurs. If brain or spinal injury causes muscles surrounding arteries to stop working, the arteries then dilate, and blood pressure drops, *neurogenic shock* occurs. If a severe allergic reaction causes the arteries to dilate, *anaphylactic shock* occurs.

SHOCK	
TYPE OF SHOCK	**MECHANISM**
Cardiogenic shock	Heart weakens, stops pumping, pumps irregularly
Hemorrhagic shock	Loss of blood internally or externally
Metabolic shock	Decrease of blood volume
Neurogenic shock	Dilation of arteries caused by damage to the brain or spine
Anaphylactic shock	Severe allergic reaction

There are many possible causes of shock, and it can be expected to occur with any major injury. Whatever the cause, shock results in insufficient movement of blood to provide adequate nutrients and oxygen to the tissues of the body. The tissues begin to suffer from the lack of nutrients and the build-up of waste products: they start to die.

The patient in the early stages of shock becomes restless and anxious as the level of oxygen delivered to the brain is lowered. The pulse rate increases as the heart labors to supply a decreased amount of blood to major organs. As the body directs blood to the important core organs and away from the periphery, the skin becomes ashen. The patient feels anxious and may be thirsty or nauseated.

In later stages of shock, the skin becomes cool and may appear blue as oxygen-depleted blood remains in these tissues and is not replaced by red oxygenated blood. As the nervous system attempts to shut down the small blood vessels in the skin, the sweat glands are also stimulated and the skin becomes damp. The respiration rate increases as the body attempts to get more oxygen to the blood. The pulse feels weak as smaller amounts of blood are pumped. The pulse becomes irregular as the heart begins to fail. With increasing damage to the brain, the pupils become sluggish or dilated. The patient becomes lethargic and slow to respond. All usual functions of the body are affected. If shock is not treated, the patient will become unconscious and death will eventually occur.

Care given during the early stages of shock may prevent further worsening of this condition and save the patient's life. If severe shock is not treated promptly, death occurs. Any patient found with severe symptoms of shock should be immediately evacuated to a hospital.

SIGNS AND SYMPTOMS OF SHOCK

EARLY SIGNS	EARLY SYMPTOMS
Restlessness	Thirstiness
Skin is pale, ashen gray, or yellowish brown	Nausea
	Anxiety
Pulse is rapid, over 100 beats/minute	
LATER SIGNS	**LATER SYMPTOMS**
Skin is cool and damp	Lethargy and apathy
Breathing may be shallow, rapid	
Pulse is weak, irregular	
Eyes become dull, pupils dilated	
Unconsciousness	

First Aid Goals. The goals of treatment are to ensure that the patient is breathing; end any obvious cause of shock, such as bleeding; reduce the energy demands on the body by maintaining body temperature; minimize pain by treating the patient gently; help the body direct blood to the core body organs and brain; and replace lost fluids.

All patients in shock should be treated gently to avoid unnecessary pain or stress and have vital signs taken frequently. Any patient who shows decreased awareness of the surroundings or decreased sensation to pain or touch should be examined carefully for other injuries.

Treatment of Shock. Treatment for shock begins early to reduce energy demands on the body, before a complete check for injuries has been finished. In a cold environment, the patient's body heat must be maintained by covering the patient. In a hot environment, the patient may need to be protected from excessive heat.

After the examination for other injuries has been completed, the patient may be positioned to assist in breathing and circulation of blood to the core organs of the body. Move the patient onto insulation if necessary. Patients having shortness of breath may be more comfortable in a semi-upright position. Circulation can be assisted by raising the legs 10 to 12 inches and keeping the head on the same level as the heart. Be sure that any leg fractures have been splinted before the legs are raised. Nauseated patients may need to be placed on their side (see pages 72-73) to prevent vomit from being drawn into the lungs (aspiration). Position the patient with as little movement as possible and avoid rough or excessive handling.

Many injuries and illnesses have signs and symptoms similar to shock. Always treat a patient who appears to have shock as if he or she is in shock. Shock's signs and symptoms, no matter what the cause, indicate potentially life-threatening conditions needing treatment and evacuation.

If the patient is to be evacuated to a hospital in a few hours, do not administer fluids or food. Fluid in the patient's stomach will be a problem if surgery is needed. If evacuation will be delayed, a lightly salted solution may be given in sips to help replace fluids. A diluted bouillon solution is an excellent fluid, as are electrolyte replacement drinks.

FIRST AID FOR SHOCK

1. Keep the patient's airway open and clear.
2. Control all obvious bleeding.
3. Treat the patient gently and minimize movement to prevent pain.
4. Maintain the patient's body temperature.

Further Treatment After the Check for Injuries Has Been Completed:

5. Position the patient to aid in the circulation of blood to the core and to aid breathing.
6. Avoid rough or excessive handling of the patient.
7. Frequently take and record the patient's vital signs.
8. Evacuate the patient as soon as possible.

Patients experiencing a great deal of emotional stress, such as observing the injury or death of a friend, may develop a condition known as psychogenic shock. **This is not true shock.** The nervous system temporarily dilates the blood vessels, and blood pools in body areas away from the brain. The patient may become agitated, confused, anxious, and speech may be slurred. Eventually the patient will faint. This condition is **not** life threatening. Unlike true shock, this condition quickly resolves when the patient faints or the emotional stress ends. The only treatment needed is to attempt to reduce the emotional stress and prevent harm from occurring.

ILLNESSES RELATED TO ENVIRONMENT: COLD, HEAT, AND HIGH ALTITUDE

Excessive heat or cold, exposure to high altitude, and overexertion may lead to many painful but usually avoidable illnesses. Prevention of these illnesses is based in a knowledge of the mechanisms leading to illness, adequate consumption of food and water, strong physical conditioning, and a continual awareness of changes taking place within and around the mountaineer.

Effects of Excessive Cold

Hypothermia

Hypothermia is a condition in which the temperature of the body's internal core has been lowered sufficiently to cause illness. Hypothermia is dangerous; it occurs without warning to the patient and quickly affects judgment and reasoning. Unless the signs and symptoms are recognized and treatment begun, hypothermia leads to apathy, collapse, and death. Hypothermia is not a condition of cold weather alone. Many hypothermia cases are reported in wet, windy weather with temperatures well above freezing. Falling in a glacial crevasse or being wetted by a cold stream can quickly bring about severe hypothermia.

It is useful to review some basic concepts of how the body can gain and lose heat. The body gains or conserves heat in four ways:

- Through the *digestion of food*. The body produces heat by digestion of food to maintain normal body temperatures.
- From the *external application of heat*. Examples of this are sun, fire, and warmth from another body.
- From *muscular activity*, either by deliberate exercise or by involuntary exercise like shivering. Shivering produces as much heat as running at a slow pace.
- Through *reduction of blood flow* near the surface of the body. Constriction of surface blood vessels reduces circulation in the

skin and blood is kept nearer to the central core of the body. Warmth is preserved for the core organs of the body: brain, heart, and lungs.

The body loses heat in the following ways:

- *Evaporation* causes the loss of a large amount of thermal energy as fluid changes into a gas. Evaporation of perspiration from the skin and fluid from the lungs during breathing contributes greatly to the amount of heat lost by the body.
- *Conduction* is the transfer of heat by direct contact. Sitting on the snow, touching cold equipment, and being rained upon are all examples of how heat can be lost as a result of conduction.
- *Radiation* is the emission of thermal energy. It causes heat loss from uncovered surfaces of the body. The head and neck, areas where large blood vessels come close to the surface of the body, are particularly susceptible to radiative heat loss.
- *Convection* is a facilitation of heat loss by the movement of air or fluid. The body continually warms, by radiation, a thin layer of air next to the skin. If the warm air remains close to the body, an insulation effect is provided. If this layer is removed by air currents, cooling takes place at a much more rapid pace.

Changes in the Body during Hypothermia. If heat loss exceeds heat gain, and this situation is allowed to continue, hypothermia results. The first response to exposure to cold is constriction of the blood vessels of the skin, and later, of the deeper-lying tissues. The effect is to decrease the amount of heat transported by blood to the skin, consequently lowering skin temperature. The cool shell of tissue now acts as an insulating layer for the deeper core areas of the body; skin temperatures may drop nearly as low as that of the surrounding environment, while the body's core temperature remains at its normal 98.6°F (37°C). If cooling continues, underlying muscles are affected and coordination is impeded. Shivering begins early after exposure to cold and becomes uncontrollable if exposure continues. With a large temperature drop on the skin's surface, the sense of touch and pain is diminished.

Signs of a reduced capacity to make judgments also appear rapidly. The patient becomes withdrawn or apathetic. As the body's core drops below 95°F (35°C), the patient may become confused and sleepy, may make poor decisions, and has further loss of coordination. Walking becomes difficult, and movements are stiff and awkward. Uncontrollable shivering may stop, and pulse and respiration may slow. As the core temperature approaches 85°F (30°C), the patient may become unconscious, and pulse and respiration will weaken or even stop. A cold heart is very sensitive. Unnecessary movement of an extremely cold patient may cause the heart to begin beating erratically or stop completely. If the patient remains cold for a number of hours, metabolic changes begin to take place in the body, particularly in the limbs. On rewarming, these changes may cause major problems for the patient, which could result in death.

Deeply hypothermic patients may recover with no permanent damage. A motionless patient, without pulse and respiration, may be revived. The patient should never be considered dead until after warming. A good rule of thumb is: "No one is dead until warm and dead." The basic goal of first aid for hypothermia is to prevent further heat loss.

Unfortunately, the signs and symptoms of hypothermia do not always conform to the severity of the condition. One patient with a low core temperature may remain conscious and rational, while another patient with little core cooling may act very confused and have great difficulty with coordination. The best sign of hypothermia is core temperature, which is measured rectally. As most mountaineers do not carry rectal thermometers, and would be unlikely to use one on all but the closest friends, the stage of hypothermia will need to be judged by other signs or symptoms. If there is any suspicion that the patient's hypothermia is either moderate or severe, then treat as if it were. A patient who is only mildly hypothermic will respond quickly to treatment, and the more aggressive treatment can be ended at that point.

Mild Hypothermia. For purposes of field treatment of hypothermia, the condition can be divided into mild and moderate-to-severe levels. The patient with mild hypothermia will complain of being cold and may develop uncontrollable shivering. As muscles in the extremities become cold, the patient experiences decreased fine motor coordination. It becomes difficult for the patient to strike a match, tie a knot, or handle a small object. The earliest sign may be a change in personality, becoming disagreeable or apathetic. The patient will have a core temperature above 90°F (32°C). Most patients with mild hypothermia will be able to rewarm once exposure to the cold has been ended.

First Aid. First aid for mild hypothermia begins with ending exposure. Get the patient out of the wind, cold, and wet. Wet clothing should be removed and replaced with dry. Increasing insulation may be sufficient to end the hypothermia, such as zipping up an open coat or putting a hat on the patient's head. Put the patient in a warm environment. Most patients will be able to return to normal without any other intervention. Additional warmth can be supplied through hot water bottles, small chemical heat packs, or other heat sources first wrapped in clothing and then placed on the chest, armpits, neck, and groin. The patient may appreciate a warm cup of soup or something to eat. Although this will not substantially warm the patient's body, it will improve the spirit. Avoid caffeine because it dilates blood vessels in the skin and may add to heat loss.

MILD HYPOTHERMIA

SIGNS AND SYMPTOMS
Complaints of cold
Shivering
Difficulty using the hands
Psychological changes, withdrawal and apathy
Core temperature above 90°F (32°C)

FIRST AID
1. End exposure—get the patient out of the cold and wet.
2. Replace wet clothing with dry, or add insulation to clothing.
3. Place the patient in a warm environment.
4. Add heat through hot-water bottles or other heat sources first wrapped in clothing.
5. Offer warm liquids or food if the patient is conscious and able to swallow easily.

Moderate to Severe Hypothermia. The moderately affected patient will show increasing lethargy and mental confusion and may refuse to recognize the illness. Uncontrollable shivering may be present or may have ceased. Speech will be slurred. The large muscles of the extremities will stiffen, and the patient will have difficulty walking or will stumble. As hypothermia deepens, the patient may become unresponsive or unconscious. The heart will also be irritable and may stop if the patient is treated roughly. The pulse and respiration decrease and may become difficult to detect. You may need to take as long as 45 to 60 seconds to detect the pulse and respiration of a hypothermic patient. The patient will have a core temperature of 90°F (32°C) or lower.

First Aid. Moderately to severely hypothermic patients are best rewarmed in the hospital under controlled conditions. Do not attempt to actively rewarm the patient if he or she can be gotten to a hospital within a few hours. End exposure to the cold. Do **not** allow the patient to walk to shelter or otherwise exercise. Such movement may force cold blood present in the limbs into the core of the body, further decreasing core temperature. Erect shelter around the patient or carry the patient to shelter. Treat the patient very gently. Replace wet clothing; wet clothing may have to be cut off. Check the patient for other injuries such as frostbite. Proceed with evacuation to a medical facility. Monitor vital signs every 15 minutes.

If a severely hypothermic patient cannot be gotten to medical care within a few hours, active rewarming should begin in the field. Rewarming of the patient should focus on delivering warmth to the head, neck, armpits, and groin areas. Warmth may be delivered by application of hot-water bottles, warmed blankets, small chemical heat packs, or another warm body. Keep hot-water bottles and chemical heat packs separated from the patient's body by a layer of cloth and monitor the temperature of the patient's skin to prevent burning the skin. Watch for signs of shock (see page 104). Evacuate the patient as soon as possible. If pulse and respiration are not found within 60 seconds, begin CPR.

MODERATE TO SEVERE HYPOTHERMIA

SIGNS AND SYMPTOMS
Lethargy, mental confusion, or refusal to recognize the problem
Slurred speech
Stumbling
Core temperature 90°F (32°C) and lower

SIGNS OF MORE SEVERE ILLNESS
Unresponsiveness
Decreased pulse and respiration
Cessation of shivering
Physical collapse

FIRST AID
If the Patient **Will Be** Evacuated Promptly:
1. End exposure—cover the patient, rather than walking the patient to shelter.
2. Treat the patient very gently.
3. Replace wet clothing with dry. Cut clothing off to prevent unnecessary movement.
4. Check the patient for other injury.
5. Evacuate the patient.

Further First Aid If the Patient **Will Not Be** Evacuated Promptly:
6. Begin active rewarming.
7. Watch for signs of shock.
8. Evacuate as soon as possible.

Prevention of Hypothermia

Prevention of hypothermia involves stopping of heat loss, termination of exposure, and early detection of signs of emerging illness.

Preventing Heat Loss. The following activities can be undertaken:

- Control evaporative heat loss by regulating clothing to prevent excessive sweating.
- Cover areas that are particularly sensitive to radiative heat loss: head, neck, and hands. Remember the old saying, "If your feet are cold put on a hat."
- Prevent convective heat loss by wearing layers of clothing, which will help to maintain the layer of warm air next to the body. Heat is lost rapidly with the lightest breeze unless this layer is maintained.
- Prevent conductive heat loss by placing insulation between the body and cold objects. A sit pad can provide significant insulation between an individual's posterior and a cold rock or patch of snow. Wetting of clothes, particularly cotton, reduces their insulative ability.
- Wear clothes that maintain their insulative properties when wet or wick wetness away from the body. Cotton pants should not be the only clothing carried by the mountaineer.
- Prevent heat loss during breathing by covering the mouth and nose with wool or other insulative material. This also helps to reduce heat loss by prewarming the air that enters the lungs.

Terminating Exposure. If you are currently warm, keep active to ensure adequate heat production. If you cannot stay dry and warm under the existing conditions, terminate exposure by getting out of the wind and rain. Bivouac early before your energy is exhausted and coordination and judgment are impaired. Eat foods high in carbohydrates that can be quickly converted to heat by the body. Avoid alcohol, which dilates surface blood vessels resulting in a sensation of warmth but an actual loss of body heat.

Early Detection. Any time a party is exposed to wind, cold, or wetness, carefully watch each individual for the signs and symptoms of hypothermia. Treatment of early hypothermia is relatively simple compared to the efforts needed to deal with a severely ill individual. The patient may deny having any problems. **Believe the signs and symptoms, not the patient.**

Cold Water Immersion

Accidental immersion in cold water can quickly result in moderate to severe hypothermia due to the high heat conductivity of water.

Blood vessels in the arms and legs are rapidly constricted, resulting in the perception of intense cold and inability to control the limbs. Patients frequently feel an immense sense of doom. Despite the perception of extreme cold, the body can conserve warmth in the core much longer than a patient might believe. Heat loss can be minimized by holding the arms crossed and the knees pulled up to the chest. This reduces the surface area of the body from which warmth can be lost to the water. Keeping as much of the body up out of the water, such as lying atop a capsized canoe, actually reduces heat loss despite the subjective perception of increased coldness due to "wind chill." Attempting to swim to shore increases the speed in which heat is lost by the body. Patients should not give up; cold water immersion is more survivable than might be believed by the patient in cold water.

First Aid. A patient of cold water immersion should be treated for hypothermia. If the patient was in the water for a short period of time, is fully conscious, and shows signs and symptoms of mild hypothermia, treat for mild hypothermia. Particular care should be taken in the rescue of the patient who has been in cold water for a longer period of time and who probably has moderate or severe hypothermia. Do not allow the patient to assist in rescue or to walk once taken from the water. Be alert for deterioration in the patient's condition, including collapse, as the cold blood kept in the extremities is returned to the body's core, further increasing hypothermia. Treat the patient for severe hypothermia and transport to medical care as soon as possible.

Frostbite and Immersion Foot

The fingers, toes, ears, and nose, which protrude from the body, are very susceptible to cooling and injury from the cold. The hands have the greatest skin area for their volume of any part of the body, and therefore cool very rapidly. If the temperature continues to drop, circulation will almost completely cease and frostbite will occur. The water in between cells freezes, and the water inside the cells moves out in response to chemical imbalances caused by the freezing. Tissues are injured physically from the expansion of the ice and by the resultant chemical imbalances within each cell. The basic goal of first aid for frostbite is to prevent further areas of damage by additional freezing or refreezing of tissue.

Superficial Frostbite. The signs and symptoms of frostbite vary in degree of severity and extent. Generally, frostbite can be divided into two categories: superficial and deep. Superficial frostbite is not as serious as deep frostbite, but it should be seen as a warning that deeper frostbite is a real risk if the condition of the patient is not improved. In superficial frostbite, only small patches of surface tissue are affected, typically on the exposed areas of the face, nose, ears, or hands. They may appear pale, dull, or waxy and will be firm to the touch. Underlying tissue will be soft. The patient may feel pain, and the area may feel intensely cold or numb.

First Aid. Place a warm body part next to the affected area and apply a firm steady pressure. Do not rub the area. Rubbing will cause damage to the already injured skin. Give ibuprofen if the body part is painful. The area should be protected from further freezing.

SUPERFICIAL FROSTBITE

SIGNS AND SYMPTOMS
Small patches of skin appear pale, dull, or waxy
Skin is firm to the touch, underlying tissue is soft
Pain may be felt
The body part may feel cold or numb

FIRST AID
Place a warm body part next to the affected area.
Do not rub the affected area.
Give ibuprofen for pain.
Protect the body part from refreezing.

Deep Frostbite. In deep frostbite, deeper tissues and more extensive areas are frozen, which may involve the hands and feet and portions of legs and arms. It is a serious problem that can result in loss of tissue or an entire body part. Early recognition of frostbite and prevention of any further injury as a result of infection, trauma, or allowing the part to thaw and refreeze is essential if the loss of tissue is to be minimized.

Skin of the affected part will be pale, dull, or waxy in appearance and will be firm. Underlying tissues will be solid. Joint movement may be limited or absent. Pain will be felt as the part freezes, and then the part will become numb and senseless. The frozen area may be as small as part of a finger or involve a whole limb.

Once a frozen part has thawed, the patient may become a stretcher case. The part will be extremely painful. Travel on a thawed foot will be almost impossible. If a frozen part accidentally thaws and refreezes, greater tissue damage will occur. Loss of a hand or foot is much more likely in the case of thawing and refreezing.

First Aid. Check for signs of hypothermia. If the patient is hypothermic, treat that first as it is life threatening. **Keep the frozen part frozen** if possible. Do not rub the frozen area as it will further damage tissue. Prevent unaffected tissue from freezing. If the part has thawed, the part should not be allowed to refreeze or bear weight. Give the patient plenty of fluids, and evacuate as soon as possible.

Thawing should be undertaken **only** if refreezing will not take place and the part can be kept under sterile conditions. This will be almost impossible to maintain in the field. To thaw a frozen part, immerse it in a water bath at 104°F (40°C) to 108°F (42°C). The bath must be kept at a constant temperature by the addition of warmed water. Rewarming at a lower temperature produces less benefit to the frozen tissues. Water hotter than 108°F may cause additional damage. A thermometer is essential for monitoring the temperature of the water. Continue the thawing until the part is completely thawed. The part should have a red or pink undertone or appear normal all the way to the end of the toes or fingers. The pink color indicates that circulation has been restored. A body part that is severely damaged may not regain complete circulation. If the pink color does not return to the limb in a reasonable amount of time, remove the part from the bath. Encourage exercise of thawed toes or fingers during and after thawing. Once thawed, position the part on a sterile pad, placing small pieces of sterile gauze between toes and fingers. Protect the thawed body part from any further damage, including rubbing caused by a sheet or blanket. Do not use hot-water bottles, heat lamps, or place the part near a hot stove, as excessive heat may cause further damage. Do not disturb blisters, since the possibility of infection is great. Take the patient to a hospital or other medical assistance. Give 400 milligrams of ibuprofen before thawing is started and every 12 hours after the initial dose. If a frozen part has accidentally thawed, protect it from further damage as you would a part that had been intentionally thawed.

DEEP FROSTBITE

SIGNS AND SYMPTOMS

Skin appears pale, dull, or waxy.

The skin is hard to the touch, underlying tissues are solid.

Joint movement is absent or restricted.

Pain may be felt as the body part freezes.

The part will become numb and senseless.

On thawing, the part will be very painful.

FIRST AID

Treat for hypothermia if present.

Keep the frozen part frozen.

Do not rub the affected part.

Prevent freezing of unaffected tissue.

If thawed, the part should **not** be allowed to refreeze or bear weight.

Give the patient plenty of fluids.

Evacuate as soon as possible.

Give 400 mg ibuprofen every 12 hours.

If Refreezing Will **Not** Take Place and the Body Part Can Be Kept Under Sterile Conditions:

Immerse the part in a water bath at 104°F (40°C) to 108°F (42°C).

Keep the bath at a constant temperature.

Continue thawing until the part has a pink undertone all the way to the tip.

Encourage exercise of thawed toes or fingers during and after thawing.

Once thawed, position the part on a sterile pad.

Place small pieces of sterile gauze between toes and fingers.

Protect blisters.

Evacuate by stretcher.

Give 400 mg ibuprofen every 12 hours.

Preventing Frostbite. The following steps can be taken:

- Wear sufficient clothing to prevent injury. Mittens are better than gloves. Face masks may be necessary in strong, cold winds.
- Clothihg should be loose enough to prevent constriction of blood vessels. Boots should not be tied tightly, and lacing should be checked frequently to ensure adequate circulation to the feet.
- An extra layer of socks should **not** be added to the feet if it will restrict circulation.
- Check to be sure that freezing and expansion of the boot liners has not impeded circulation.
- Special care should be taken with any rigid boot that swelling of the feet does not impair circulation.
- Do not touch cold metals with bare skin as heat is conducted quickly away.
- Do not touch gasoline with the bare skin. The rapid evaporation of gasoline may quickly lead to frozen tissues.
- Exercise the toes and fingers to help maintain circulation.
- Observe the conditions of your partner's face, hands, and ears frequently for any indication of superficial frostbite.
- Avoid smoking and caffeine before and during exposure to cold.
- Individuals with histories of circulatory problems should be especially careful in taking necessary measures to prevent frostbite.

Immersion Foot. Immersion foot occurs when the extremity has been exposed to cold (32° to 50°F), wet weather for a long period of time. Tissues do not freeze, but damage to the circulatory and nervous systems takes place. The foot is cold, swollen, mottled in color, and may be waxy to the touch. The patient may complain of numbness and pain. Treatment includes ending exposure, drying the feet, giving ibuprofen every 6 hours, and evacuation to medical care. Be sure that the patient receives adequate food and liquids. Prevention focuses on keeping feet dry and managing boots and socks so that swelling does not impede circulation in the feet.

Effects of Excessive Heat

The body reacts to an increase in temperature in two ways: by dilating the skin's blood vessels, allowing more blood to pass near the surface to be cooled; and by increased sweating. Sweating results in the loss of water and electrolytes (salts) as well as cooling by evaporation. Thirst is not a reliable indicator of the need for water and will usually not occur until the body has lost about 1 quart. Elevated body temperature and excessive loss of electrolytes and water can result in a number of heat-related illnesses.

Heat Cramps and Fainting

Muscular cramps in the limbs or abdomen may result from exposure to high temperatures and humidity combined with physical exercise or by loss of electrolytes. Resting, massaging, and stretching the muscle may reduce the spasm. Give the patient lightly salted water or a commercially made electrolyte replacement solution and avoid further strenuous exercise.

Fainting in a hot environment may result from the pooling of blood in the legs. Patients usually recover quickly after collapse. Allow the patient to rest in a shaded area and offer the patient water, a slightly salty liquid, or an electrolyte replacement drink.

Heat Exhaustion

Heat exhaustion usually occurs in individuals who lose large amounts of sweat while exercising. Heat exhaustion may occur during warm weather, but the weather need not be hot. Cross-country snow skiers can experience heat exhaustion if adequate water and electrolytes have not been consumed during a hard day trip. Dehydration is a major factor in the development of heat exhaustion. Loss of electrolytes can also be a factor in heat exhaustion.

The patient's skin may be damp with profuse sweat. The skin temperature will be normal, slightly warm, or cool. The patient's oral temperature and pulse rate will be slightly elevated. The patient may report nausea, general muscular weakness, dizziness, thirst, or headache.

First Aid. The first step is to get the patient into a cooler, shady environment. Fluids should be given in small sips because the patient may be nauseated. Salted water may add to that discomfort. Flavoring the water may help to reduce the chance of vomiting. Once the patient has cooled down, replacement of electrolytes may be undertaken by giving bouillon, other salty foods, or an electrolyte replacement drink. Once the patient has fully recovered, travel or activity may be resumed. Depending on the extent of illness, recovery may take 24 hours. The patient should be observed for recurrence of heat exhaustion for the rest of the trip.

HEAT EXHAUSTION

SIGNS AND SYMPTOMS
Sweating—usually profuse
Skin temperature normal, slightly cool, or warm
Oral temperature normal or slightly elevated
Pulse rate slightly elevated
Sensation of nausea, weakness, dizziness, thirst, or headache
Signs and symptoms resolve quickly after treatment begins

FIRST AID
Place the patient in a cool, shady environment.
Give the patient water in sips.
Resume activity after all signs and symptoms are
    completely gone.
Observe the patient for recurrence of heat exhaustion.

Heatstroke

Heatstroke is a life-threatening condition that can quickly lead to collapse and death. In heatstroke, the body's internal temperature is usually above 105°F (41°C). Individuals resuming an active sport after a long period of inactivity, or exercising in a hot and humid environment to which they are not accustomed, are particularly susceptible to heatstroke. Their skin will appear initially damp, and relatively cool, although their internal temperature is dangerously high. The most apparent sign of heatstroke for these patients is an irrational change in their behavior; they may become confused or combative and aggressive. They may have difficulty walking or collapse physically. Later, the patient's skin may become red and dry. These patients are experiencing *exertional heatstroke*.

The heat illness most frequently reported in general first aid books, *classic heatstroke,* will probably not be found in mountaineers. The most common victims of classic heatstroke are urban, elderly, obese, or alcoholic. In classic heatstroke, the patient's skin is usually red, hot, and dry to the touch. The common signs of both types of heatstroke are an extremely high internal temperature and an elevated pulse rate. Both types share symptoms of weakness, dizziness, and headache.

Persistent signs of cardiovascular shock (see page 104), psychological changes, and high internal temperatures distinguish heatstroke from heat exhaustion. Mental changes and symptoms of shock resolve quickly if the patient is experiencing heat exhaustion and receives treatment.

First Aid. The goal of treatment for heatstroke is to reduce body temperature immediately. Remove or loosen tight clothing, and place the patient in a cool, shady environment. Apply wet cloths or cool water to the head, neck, armpits, and groin. Vigorous fanning will help the cooling. If you notice the patient begin to shiver, stop cooling efforts immediately. Monitor the patient carefully after cooling for any indication of a rebound increase in temperature. If the patient is conscious, give water in sips. The patient has experienced a serious illness, must be carried out, and needs hospitalization. The patient must not be allowed to walk or resume any activity.

HEATSTROKE

SIGNS AND SYMPTOMS

Irrational, confused, or combative behavior

Unconsciousness

Skin: Damp, relatively cool that may later become red and dry—**exertional heatstroke**

OR

Red, dry, hot skin—**classic heatstroke**

Difficulty walking

Elevated pulse rate

Sensation of nausea, weakness, dizziness, thirst, or headache

Internal temperature greater than 105°F (41°C)

Signs and symptoms persist after treatment has begun

FIRST AID

Decrease body temperature immediately:
a. Remove or loosen tight clothing.
b. Place patient in a cool, shady environment.
c. Cool the patient with wet cloths or cool water.

Immediately stop efforts at cooling if shivering occurs.

Monitor the patient carefully.

Give water in sips to a conscious patient.

Evacuate by stretcher from mountaineering settings as soon as possible.

Prevention of Heat-Related Illnesses. The following steps can be taken:
- Drink large amounts of water, even when thirst does not indicate a need. Water stops should be scheduled, even in cool weather or at high altitude. Between one and two cups of water should be drunk every hour of activity.
- Regulate activity to time of day, temperature, and condition of the party to avoid unnecessary exposure to heat stress.
- Taking salt tablets is **not** recommended.

Prevention of heat injuries is based on adequate consumption of water and electrolytes. Table salt should not be taken in large amounts unless water is freely available. The amount of electrolytes obtained in the usual diet is sufficient for most individuals even in the hottest weather. Some individuals may feel better in hot weather with a slight increase in table salt consumption. Hikers may wish to carry pretzels or some other salty snack to nibble while on the trail. Flavored powders containing electrolytes added to water may be used to replace electrolytes lost to sweat. Directions must be carefully followed in mixing these powders. Highly concentrated solutions will impair the ability of the stomach to absorb the fluid or electrolytes.

Effects of High Altitude

High altitude illnesses are related to the body's attempts to compensate for hypoxia, decreased levels of oxygen in the body, which is the result of decreased oxygen available at altitudes over 2,500 meters (8,202 feet). Occasionally, altitudes of 1,500 meters (4,921 feet) bring on mild symptoms for some people. Above 3,500 meters (11,483 feet), the percentage of oxygen in the blood drops significantly below its ability to carry oxygen. Severe high-altitude-related illnesses are most common at or above this altitude.

The actual altitude reached, how quickly that altitude was gained, and individual physiology all contribute to a mountaineer's reaction to high altitude. Some will adjust quickly to high altitude or will quickly overcome mild illness. A few individuals will not acclimatize, even if they increase their exposure gradually. Others will not be affected at much higher altitudes. The healthy, well-conditioned athlete may experience high altitude illness as frequently as the out-of-shape novice. High altitude problems can strike individuals already acclimatized. High altitude illness can be a nuisance or a life-threatening problem if not treated quickly. High altitude illnesses strike unpredictably; mountaineers must not minimize the early symptoms of illness, which are similar to those of just being tired.

Increased rate and depth of breathing (ventilation) is an early adaptation to high altitude. It increases oxygen delivery to the body and reduces carbon dioxide in the lungs. This response is controlled by a physiological sensor in the circulatory system that has variable response rates in different individuals. Some individuals, despite high levels of physical conditioning, may not experience increased rates of ventilation as quickly as others, thus reducing their ability to acclimatize. Other changes in the body act to slow down increased ventilation, but ventilation generally tends to increase at high altitude, reaching a maximum at four to seven days.

Complex changes in the circulatory system also occur, with an initial increase in pulse rate and changes to the pressure of the blood circulating through the heart, lungs, and brain. The blood vessels in the brain may dilate, resulting in headaches. Despite decreased availability of oxygen with high altitude, the body usually is able to maintain adequate levels of oxygen in the heart, lungs, and brain. Changes in the blood itself occur with an increase in the concentration of hemoglobin in the blood, as well as in the production of red blood cells. Hemoglobin is the substance which carries oxygen in red blood cells. Although an increased concentration of hemoglobin does not decrease susceptibility to illness when initially exposed to high altitude, it will increase the availability of oxygen to the body over time and may result in improved acclimatization.

Sleep is disturbed at high altitude, with more time spent awake and changes to breathing during sleep for over 80 percent of individuals. The ability to exercise is decreased with increasing altitude. As you ascend, the body's ability to get oxygen into the blood decreases, so that with even a few steps, a mountaineer will feel breathless and need to stop to allow ventilation to bring more oxygen into the body.

At extreme altitude, over 5,500 meters (18,045 feet), the body is no longer able to overcome the lack of oxygen. Although mountaineers can survive brief exposures to these altitudes, they cannot acclimatize, and must return to lower altitudes or die.

The body's reaction to high altitude is complex. No one change alone is the reason for the experience of high-altitude-related illness. No single intervention has proven effective at preventing illnesses. Even the most careful attempt to acclimatize to high altitude through graded ascent and sleeping at the lowest possible altitude, which is the best preventive action, cannot prevent all experiences of high-altitude-related problems.

High-altitude-related illnesses are commonly divided into Acute Mountain Sickness (AMSC), High Altitude Pulmonary Edema (HAPE), and High Altitude Cerebral Edema (HACE). The primary first aid for all moderate or severe high altitude problems is **descent** to lower altitudes.

Acute Mountain Sickness

The signs and symptoms of Acute Mountain Sickness vary greatly in their severity. Symptoms may take as little as 6 hours or up to several days to develop after the mountaineer has reached high altitude. Minor symptoms may disappear if the mountaineer remains at high altitude.

The patient may experience difficulty sleeping and have an unusual pattern of breathing during sleep: the patient may stop breathing for several seconds, then take several rapid breaths, and then repeat this pattern. The affected mountaineer may have swollen hands and feet. The patient will feel "rotten," with fatigue, headache, muscular weakness or pain, nausea, dizziness, and shortness of breath. The increased urination associated with achieving high altitude may not be present. Moderate symptoms include a headache that will not respond to aspirin or ibuprofen, and vomiting. Severe signs include difficulty with walking and coordination, changes in personality such as combativeness or impaired judgment, and severe shortness of breath while at rest or during minimal activity. Moderate to severe symptoms indicate that the patient is significantly ill and requires immediate care.

First Aid. The patient should make a conscious effort to breathe deeply and regularly, perhaps through pursed lips. This will increase the oxygen taken into the body. Breathing too rapidly (hyperventilation) can lead to dizziness or nausea. Do not go any higher until signs and symptoms have ended. If you must continue travel, the pace should be slower. Stop if symptoms make travel difficult. At high altitude, dehydration is a threat and can worsen AMS. Make sure the patient drinks plenty of fluids. Aspirin or ibuprofen can be taken for headache. Avoid any medication containing codeine or other narcotics as they depress breathing and will worsen AMS.

Any symptom that persists for more than 24 hours or the presence of **any** moderate to severe symptom or sign, such as vomiting, severe headache, difficulty walking, or severe shortness of breath, should be cause for undertaking the primary first aid—**descent** to lower altitude.

Several drugs, including acetazolamide and dexamethasone, have been shown to be useful in the prevention and treatment of AMS. Acetazolamide speeds the body's acclimatization to high altitude, lessens unusual breathing patterns during sleep, and consequently reduces the risk of experiencing AMS. However, it has uncomfortable side effects, such as tingling of fingers and toes, nausea, and drowsiness. Acetazolamide also increases fluid loss, and the mountaineer taking this drug should drink extra fluids to prevent dehydration. Dexamethasone has been found to prevent and reduce the symptoms of AMS. It also seems to cause a euphoric feeling, which masks symptoms of AMS. Because of dexamethasone's potential for long-term severe side effects, it should be reserved for individuals unable to take acetazolamide, individuals who do not respond to acetazolamide, or those who are required to ascend to high altitudes quickly as part of search-and-rescue efforts. Nifedipine may also be useful in preventing HAPE. These drugs should be taken only under a physician's direction and are **not recommended for routine use.** Sleeping pills and narcotic pain medications for management of high-altitude-associated headache **must be avoided** as they reduce the body's drive to breathe.

ACUTE MOUNTAIN SICKNESS (AMS)

MILD AMS

Signs and Symptoms	First Aid
Difficulty with sleep	Breathe deeply and regularly.
Unusual breathing during sleep	Stop ascent until signs and
Swelling in hands and face	symptoms disappear.
Headache, mild to severe	Increase intake of fluids.
Fatigue and weakness	Aspirin or ibuprofen may be
Lack of appetite, nausea	taken for headache.
Dizziness	Rest if symptoms make
Shortness of breath	travel difficult.
	DESCEND if signs and
	symptoms are severe or do
	not resolve in 24 hours.

MODERATE AMS

Signs and Symptoms	First Aid
Signs and symptoms of MILD AMS	Breathe deeply and regularly.
Vomiting	Increase intake of fluids.
Headache does not respond to	Aspirin or ibuprofen may be
aspirin or ibuprofen	taken for headache.
	DESCEND IMMEDIATELY and
	seek medical help.

SEVERE AMS

Signs and Symptoms	First Aid
Signs and symptoms of	Breathe deeply and regularly.
MODERATE AMS	Increase intake of fluids.
Difficulty with walking and	Aspirin or ibuprofen may be
coordination	taken for headache.
Combativeness	**DESCEND IMMEDIATELY** and
Severe shortness of breath,	seek medical help.
even at rest	

High Altitude Pulmonary Edema

Pulmonary edema is a leakage of fluid into the lungs, making breathing difficult. It is a serious condition that requires rapid identification and treatment. HAPE may be seen at altitudes as low as 8,000 feet (2,438 meters), and it is associated with rapid ascent and immediate physical exertion upon arrival at high altitude. The first cases were described as "skiers' pneumonia," as they were found in lowland individuals who began skiing immediately after flying to resorts above 10,000 feet (3,048 meters).

Onset of symptoms are not immediate, taking at least 6 to 8 hours to develop. Most instances of HAPE occur after two days at high altitude. Early symptoms may resemble AMS; headache, nausea, lack of appetite, dizziness, shortness of breath, and general weakness or fatigue. Later signs and symptoms are related to the filling of the lungs with fluid and are often accompanied by a great sense of anxiety as breathing becomes progressively more difficult. The patient will not want to lay flat. The pulse will be very rapid, even at rest. The patient will feel extremely short of breath and have difficulty with any exertion. Any persistent cough, at rest or during exercise, may be an indication of pulmonary edema. The cough will be dry at first, and later produce watery pink sputum. Gurgling or crackling sounds may be heard in the lungs. Respiration will be rapid, 30 or more per minute in severe cases. During the night, the patient may wake up with extreme difficulty breathing. In later stages, the patient may become incoherent and experience hallucinations. Without descent, the patient will drop into a coma with death following in 6 to 12 hours.

First Aid. The primary first aid for HAPE is **descent, descent, descent.** A descent of 1,000 feet will bring great improvement in the patient's condition. When descent is impossible, supplemental oxygen may be given by trained rescuers. A mask that provides resistance to airflow on exhalation has also been used to increase the percent of oxygen kept in the lungs. Portable hyperbaric chambers, consisting of a flexible bag in which the patient is placed and a pumping system that allows the air pressure in the bag to be artificially increased, also improve the oxygen level in the body. Increasing the intake of oxygen mimics descent to lower altitude. Signs and symptoms will return if the patient is removed from the bag and will persist if the patient is **not** removed to lower altitude. Administration of drugs, acetazolamide and nifedipine, by trained individuals may also be included in treatment. **Descent** is the only cure for HAPE. As soon as descent is possible, the patient must be assisted down. **Attempts to extend the stay at high altitude by use of oxygen, breathing devices, or drugs may threaten the life of the patient.**

HIGH ALTITUDE PULMONARY EDEMA

SIGNS	SYMPTOMS
Very rapid pulse	Headache
Gurgling sounds in lungs	Nausea and lack of appetite
Very rapid respiration rate	Dizziness
Dry cough at first, becoming wet	Weakness and fatigue
Incoherence or hallucinations	Increasing anxiety
	Shortness of breath

FIRST AID

1. Descend.
2. Descend.
3. Descend to lower altitude at the first indication of pulmonary edema.
4. If descent is not possible, carefully monitor the patient for breathing difficulties. Oxygen and a hyperbaric chamber may reduce signs and symptoms.
5. Assist breathing as necessary.

High Altitude Cerebral Edema

HACE is a relatively rare condition in which the brain swells. HACE takes several days after arrival at high altitude to develop, although occasional cases have been reported as developing shortly after arrival at high altitude. The earliest signs and symptoms include difficulty with walking and balance and psychological withdrawal. The patient

HIGH ALTITUDE CEREBRAL EDEMA

EARLY SIGNS AND SYMPTOMS	LATER SIGNS AND SYMPTOMS
Difficulty with walking and balance	Disorientation and confusion
Psychological withdrawal	Hallucinations
	Headache
	Nausea
	Vomiting

FIRST AID

1. Descend.
2. Descend.
3. Descend.
4. If descent is not possible, carefully monitor the patient for breathing difficulties. Oxygen and a hyperbaric chamber may reduce signs and symptoms.

may lie in a tent, not getting up to take meals, not speaking, not even going out to urinate. The patient will become disoriented, confused, and have hallucinations. Headache, nausea, and vomiting will probably precede more severe symptoms. A simple test for early cerebral edema is to ask the patient to follow a straight line walking heel-to-toe. If the patient loses balance or begins to fall, cerebral edema must be suspected.

If **descent** to lower altitude does not occur, the patient will lapse into coma. If descent is impossible, supplemental oxygen, use of a hyperbaric chamber, and administration of dexamethasone by trained individuals may be helpful. The party should not wait for rescue or other help if descent is at all possible. With any indication of possible cerebral edema, descent **must** be undertaken.

Prevention of High Altitude Illnesses. The following steps can be taken:

- Ascend to high altitude in stages, allowing the body time to acclimatize.
- Climb slowly. Above 10,000 feet (3,048 meters) it is wise to allow 1 day per 1,000 feet (305 meters) of elevation gained for acclimatization.
- Once reaching high altitude, rest is essential. Only light physical exercise should be performed for the first 24 hours.
- If climbing a number of summits or hauling loads on one mountain, descend to the lowest possible level for sleep. "Climb high, sleep low."
- Consume sufficient water to prevent dehydration; you must drink much more than needed to slake thirst.
- Eat sufficient food to maintain energy levels. Carbohydrates should be the major part of food consumed. A diet of at least 70 percent carbohydrates can reduce symptoms of AMS at altitudes above 16,000 feet.
- At the first sign of severe headache not relieved by aspirin or ibuprofen, persistent coughing, vomiting, loss of coordination, or mental confusion, descend to lower altitude.
- Avoid alcohol, caffeine, narcotic pain killers, and sleeping pills, as they tend to either dehydrate the body or interfere with respiratory drive.
- Pregnant women should consult their physicians regarding any possible complications that might result from exposure to high altitude.

The Human Body under Stress

This section has dealt with illnesses experienced from stresses placed on the human body. Heat, cold, and high altitude all require adaptations by the body to maintain normal levels of functioning. Adaptation requires energy, gained from food and water, aided by adequate rest and physical conditioning. If that energy is not available, the individual will become sick in some fashion. It is not surprising that many of the illnesses discussed in this section resemble fatigue at their onset and that their symptoms are reduced by eating food and drinking water.

Heavy physical activity increases the body's need for energy and water. An average adult requires approximately 5,000 calories per day for heavy activity. To accomplish this, a conscientious intake of food should be maintained in small quantities every hour. Diets should contain large quantities of carbohydrates, which are quickly converted into glucose and carried into the bloodstream. But they should not be eaten to the exclusion of fatty foods and proteins. Fats and proteins take considerably longer to digest, but they are important for providing long-term energy.

As the body exerts itself and heat builds, it perspires. During strenuous activity, particularly at high altitude, the amount of fluids lost through perspiration and evaporation of moisture from the lungs may be as much as 5 quarts or more per day. If a substantial amount of fluid is lost and not replaced, the body's chemical equilibrium is upset and illness is more likely to occur. Fluid intake for a 12-hour day of moderate activity should be at least 2 quarts in temperate climates. Fluid intake for a longer climb or for more strenuous activity should be from 2 to 5 quarts. Enough water should be drunk to keep the urine clear and straw colored. The body **cannot** continue without adequate fluids, as it can without food, for more than a few hours or days.

The efficiency with which energy can be used by the body is related to physical conditioning and fatigue. The greater the level of physical conditioning, the greater efficiency with which food and water are used by the body. Consequently, greater physical conditioning is related to decreased susceptibility to illnesses such as hypothermia and frostbite. A fatigued mountaineer is more likely to experience difficulties with heat or cold than a well-rested, well-fed mountaineer. Prevention of many of the environmentally related illnesses is related to the body's ability to use food and water in an efficient manner to combat the stresses of heat, cold, and high altitude. Adequate consumption of food and water, sufficient rest, and a good level of physical conditioning are essential components of prevention of environmentally related illness.

SUDDEN MAJOR ILLNESS

Sudden major illness, such as heart attack, is relatively rare in the mountaineering setting. However, the ability to recognize and then aid a patient of a sudden illness can literally mean the difference between life and death.

Difficulty Breathing

Difficulty breathing, or "shortness of breath," is the subjective sensation of not getting enough air. The patient may additionally have objective signs, such as a rapid breathing rate or the ability to speak in short phrases only.

There are a variety of reasons for the sudden appearance of difficulty breathing, ranging from the unexpected worsening of some longstanding disease, such as asthma, to some totally new process occurring within the body. The most likely causes in the backcountry are an allergic reaction or a partial obstruction of the airway, as from a piece of fruit or cheese.

The patient of an acute asthma attack will usually have had one before and know what is happening. Similarly, the patient of an allergic reaction may also be aware of having the existing medical condition known as "hypersensitivity." On the other hand, although the patient of a partial obstruction of the airway may be aware of what is happening, he or she may not be able to tell you whether the airway is blocked because the patient can't talk.

First Aid. Anyone with major breathing difficulty should be evacuated as soon as possible, by self-evacuation when feasible. People who are having difficulty breathing are usually more comfortable sitting up. Patients of *asthma attacks* will benefit from a calm approach. Individuals with known asthma frequently carry medication in the form of inhalers, pills, or injectable solutions. A first aider may assist the patient in the administration of this medication.

Any individual who experiences difficulty breathing caused by an allergic reaction to being bitten or stung must be evacuated immediately because of the problem in predicting whether the condition will worsen. First aid for allergic reactions are found in a later section. First aid for an obstructed airway was discussed in Chapter 2 (see page 39): if the patient is not moving air in or out, then start the abdominal thrusts.

DIFFICULTY BREATHING

CAUSES

Worsening of a disease, such as asthma

Allergic reaction

Partial obstruction of the airway

SIGNS AND SYMPTOMS

Shortness of breath

Rapid breathing rate

Ability to speak in short phrases only

FIRST AID

Remain calm.

Assist the patient to a comfortable position.

Assist the patient with medication.

Evacuate as soon as possible, by self-evacuation when feasible.

Treat the obstructed airway as described earlier.

Chest Pain

Chest pain can be described as "sharp," "squeezing," "crushing," "tightness," and so on. The most common cause of chest pain is heart disease, but in a mountaineering setting it is more likely due to a chest injury (rib fracture). Other possible causes include a spontaneous collapsed lung (pneumothorax, see page 82), which occasionally occurs in young people who are exercising heavily. The pain from a spontaneous collapsed lung is usually sharp, confined to a small area, and is associated with anxiety and difficulty breathing.

Usually the patient of heart disease is aware of the problem, although many patients of a heart attack will deny the seriousness of the pain. The pain from a heart attack may radiate down the left arm and be associated with an irregular pulse and cool, clammy skin. Some heart disease patients have angina, which is chest pain that comes on with exertion, cold, or emotional stress. Unlike heart attack, angina is generally relieved by rest, and rarely lasts more than 10 minutes.

First Aid. Most patients with chest pain are more comfortable sitting up. The patient of a heart attack should be placed in a semi-reclining position and monitored closely for signs of shock (see page 104) or possible sudden cardiac arrest. If shock occurs, raise the patient's legs 10 to 12 inches; if the heart stops, start CPR (see pages 39–41). Often the patient with heart disease will have medications that a physician has prescribed. You can assist the patient with the medication.

The patient of a spontaneous collapsed lung may be more comfortable lying down on the affected side. The patient may be able to walk out if someone else carries the patient's pack and the trail is downhill.

Any patient with serious chest pain needs to be evacuated as soon as possible. If the pain is reduced after rest, the patient may be assisted in a self-evacuation. If chest pain returns with exercise, then the patient must stop all activity and be evacuated by stretcher.

CHEST PAIN

CAUSES
Heart disease
Rib fracture
Spontaneous collapsed lung (Pneumothorax)

SIGNS AND SYMPTOMS
Pain in the chest
Pain radiating down the left arm
Denial of the seriousness of the pain
Signs of shock—irregular pulse and cool, clammy skin

FIRST AID
Remain calm.
Assist the patient to a comfortable position.
Assist the patient with medication.
Allow the patient to rest.
Monitor for signs of shock or possible sudden cardiac arrest.
Treat for shock or begin CPR if necessary.
Evacuate as soon as possible, by self-evacuation if pain
    does not return on exercise.

Unconsciousness

Unconsciousness can result from either sudden illness, injury, or both together. A thorough head-to-toe examination is important. Causes include head injury, stroke, shock, epileptic seizure, diabetic emergency, asphyxia (oxygen deprivation), and heatstroke.

A *head injury* may be obvious from the appearance or history of what happened (see page 71). The *stroke* patient may initially have had a severe headache and may have paralysis on one side. The patient in *shock* will have a fast pulse and cool, clammy skin (see page 104). An *epileptic seizure,* or convulsion, generally lasts about 2 minutes and is most often followed by about 5 minutes of unconsciousness. *Diabetic* patients often have medical identification bracelets. *Asphyxia* (oxygen deprivation) may be obvious (as in a drowning patient) or not (as in carbon monoxide poisoning, which can occur when cooking in a snow cave or tent without ventilation).

First Aid. The number-one priority with an unconscious patient is to make sure that the **airway** is open. Once the airway is assured, do the head-to-toe exam. Remember that all unconscious injury patients are assumed to have a neck injury until proven otherwise, so immobilize the spine. The unconscious, uninjured patient can be positioned on his or her side to help maintain an open airway. All unconscious patients will need to be evacuated as soon as possible. Monitor the patient's vital signs frequently.

Head injury, shock, and heatstroke were discussed previously (see pages 71, 102, 118, respectively). First aid for asphyxia consists of providing good air and artificial respiration when necessary.

First aid for a *diabetic emergency* actually consists of doing something before the patient becomes unconscious. The diabetic patient can have problems when there is an imbalance between food intake, exercise, and insulin. Two conditions can result: high blood sugar or low blood sugar. High blood sugar is characterized by a gradual onset and dry, red skin. Low blood sugar is characterized by rapid onset and pale, moist skin. The diabetic may recognize the signs and know what to do; but, if the patient is confused or disoriented, first aid always consists of giving the patient sugar. If the patient does not start feeling better in 5 minutes, additional medical help may be needed. If the patient becomes unconscious, place the patient on his or her side. Small amounts of sugar in the form of crushed hard candy can be placed inside the cheek and allowed to dissolve, repeatedly. An unconscious diabetic patient needs to be evacuated.

Eye Care. If the patient is unconscious for more than 1 hour, do the following to protect the eyes. Keep the eyelids closed to slow drying of the surface of the eye and to prevent scratching of the eyeball.

The unconscious patient with contact lenses will need to have the contacts removed. When the eyes are kept closed continuously, without blinking, for long periods of time, the moisture normally present gradually disappears. Without moisture, less oxygen can get to the surface of the eye, and damage can result. Even soft contact lenses, which under normal circumstances readily allow moisture and oxygen to pass through, can dry out and adhere to the surface. (See page 58 for instructions on contact lens removal.)

UNCONSCIOUSNESS

CAUSES
Head injury
Stroke
Epileptic seizure
Diabetic emergency
Asphyxia (oxygen deprivation)
Heatstroke
Shock

FIRST AID
Ensure that the airway is open.
Check for other injuries—look for specific causes.
Immobilize the spine unless neck and back injury can be ruled out.
Monitor vital signs frequently.
Evacuate as soon as possible.
Remove contacts from a patient who is unconscious for 1 hour or longer.
Treat for specific conditions (head injury, etc.) if suspected.

Allergic Reactions

Allergic reactions occur when the body reacts to the presence of a foreign substance. Severe allergic reactions kill twice as many people each year as snakebites. Foreign substances can enter the body in a number of different ways: with an insect bite or sting, as from a wasp or a bee; through inhalation, as of pollen; or in food, such as nuts. The seriousness of an allergic reaction can vary from mild symptoms of itching and burning to severe anaphylactic shock (see page 103). It is difficult to predict which patients of allergic reaction will progress to severe shock.

Most people with allergies are aware of this problem, and they often wear medical identification bracelets. The patient having an allergic reaction may first be aware of a generalized warmth and itching, particularly of the hands and feet. The next symptom may be difficulty breathing, and signs such as a rash, hives, and wheezing may appear. Swelling of the lips, tongue, eyelids, and hands may follow. The signs of shock (rapid, weak pulse; pale, cool, clammy skin) will be late findings and signify a poor prognosis in a mountaineering setting.

First Aid. First aid for an allergic reaction includes remaining calm, assisting the patient in the administration of medication, monitoring the patient's condition, and evacuation. Allergic reactions to additional exposure to the foreign substance will be reduced by taking diphenhydramine, an over-the-counter antihistamine. The usual dosage for an adult is 25 to 50 milligrams every 4 to 6 hours. This drug does have significant potential side effects, including drowsiness. Many people with known allergies or asthma carry inhalers that can be used to reduce breathing problems.

Severe difficulties with breathing or symptoms of shock related to allergic reactions require the use of an injectable prescription medication, epinephrine. Small kits that contain syringes of epinephrine, or a device resembling a small pen that delivers epinephrine to a patient, are available on a prescription basis. If the patient has prescribed medications, it is appropriate to assist the patient in taking them.

The patient of an allergic reaction that includes even the **slightest** difficulty breathing should be evacuated as soon as possible. Evacuation should not be delayed by waiting to see if the reaction gets worse.

ALLERGIC REACTIONS

CAUSES
Exposure to pollens, foods, plants, drugs, or insects to which the patient is sensitive

SIGNS AND SYMPTOMS
Sensation of generalized warmth and itching in hands and feet
Difficulty breathing
Rash
Hives
Wheezing
Swelling of the lips, tongue, eyelids, and hands
Signs of shock

FIRST AID
Remain calm.
Assist the patient in the administration of medication.
Monitor the patient's condition.
Give diphenhydramine—25 to 50 mg every 4 to 6 hours for an adult.
Evacuate.

MAJOR BITES AND STINGS
Snakebites

Of the 7,000 people bitten by snakes each year in the United States, fewer than fifteen die. In at least 22 percent of bites from poisonous snakes no venom is injected. The seriousness of a snake envenomation is related to the amount of venom injected, the location of the bite, the type of snake, and the age and general health of the patient. Bites limited to the superficial tissues are less severe than bites that reach deep into muscles or that are near blood vessels.

The United States has two main families of venomous snakes. Pit vipers, found throughout the United States, include rattlesnakes, copperheads, and cottonmouths and are identified by vertical elliptical pupils, a triangular-shaped head, and by a small pit below and in front of the eye. Signs and symptoms of envenomation include one or more fang marks, localized pain, and swelling that may include the full limb. Nausea, vomiting, and tingling occur with moderate envenomation. Serious envenomation may result in shock (see page 102), coma, and paralysis, which take a number of hours to occur.

Coral snakes are found in the south and southwestern United States. They have characteristic bands of red, black, and yellow or white encircling the body. Other snakes have the same colors, but only coral snakes have red butting on yellow or white. The venom of coral snakes affects the nervous system and is considered more dangerous than the venom of pit vipers. Luckily, only 40 percent of bites from coral snakes result in envenomation. Signs and symptoms may take up to 12 hours to appear and include tremors, drowsiness, and slurred speech. Severe envenomation may result in respiratory and cardiac failure.

First Aid. Avoid panic. Excitement and hysteria alone can result in reactions such as nausea and dizziness, making it difficult to determine if the bite was from a poisonous or nonpoisonous snake. Gently cleanse the wound and apply a sterile dressing. Immobilize the bitten limb by splinting as if it were fractured, and keep it lower than the heart. Keep the patient's physical activity to a minimum. Obtain medical assistance.

If rescue can be obtained by walking a short distance and the symptoms are minor, the patient may walk out slowly, taking frequent rests. If rescue involves hours of hiking or severe symptoms develop, the patient should be kept at rest while a partner goes out for help. One device, the Extractor, has been found to remove significant amounts of venom without any incision of the skin if used within a few minutes of the bite. Identification of the type of snake may aid in medical treatment given to the patient. Incision and sucking, tourniquets or constricting bands, cold therapy, and electric shocks have **not** been found to be effective and cause unnecessary damage.

SNAKEBITES

SIGNS AND SYMPTOMS

One or more fang marks

Localized pain

Swelling that may include the full limb

Nausea

Vomiting

Tingling

Neurological changes—tremors, drowsiness, and slurred speech

Severe envenomation—shock, coma, paralysis, respiratory or cardiac failure

Signs and symptoms may take up to 12 hours to appear

FIRST AID

Remain calm.

Cleanse the wound.

Apply a sterile dressing.

Immobilize the bitten part with a splint.

Keep the bitten area lower than the heart.

Minimize the patient's physical activity.

Evacuate as soon as possible.

Self-evacuate if the distance is short and symptoms are minor.

Identify the type of snake.

Prevention. Snakes are generally not aggressive and will bite only when threatened. Never place your hand or foot into places you cannot first see (this includes climbing holds in desert areas). As the majority of snakebites are on hands, lower legs, and feet, protective clothing can prevent envenomations. Leather gloves and boots and sturdy trousers should be worn while traveling in snake-infested areas.

Arthropod Stings and Bites

Stinging Insects. Reactions to bee and wasp stings or mosquito and fly bites are usually localized to the site of the bite. Stings to the inside of the nose or mouth may cause breathing difficulties and become true emergencies. First aid includes rapid removal of the stinging apparatus by scraping it off the skin or squeezing, if necessary. Apply ice to reduce swelling. Multiple stings may cause more severe reactions and require medical attention. Stings and bites of centipedes and millipedes may be more serious, but these creatures are found in exotic locations and are infrequently encountered. Severe allergic reactions to wasp and bee stings were discussed in an earlier section.

Spider Bites. Bites of brown recluse spiders cause the greatest problems of any spiders in the United States. These spiders are most commonly found in hot climates. Bites usually occur at night from spiders trapped in bedding. At the time of the bite there is usually nothing more than transient irritation. A blister or ulcer develops 6 to 12 hours later, which may progress over a number of days to serious damage to underlying muscle. There is no first aid for this type of bite other than recognizing and reporting it to a physician and keeping the wound clean and covered with a dressing until help is obtained.

Black widow spiders are found throughout the United States except Alaska. Female spiders are noted by a red marking in the shape of an hourglass on the abdomen. They frequently hide in dark areas such as outhouses. Muscle spasms and cramps are experienced within 1 hour of a bite. More severe reactions include tingling and burning sensations, headache, dizziness, vomiting, and difficulty breathing. Signs and symptoms usually end within 48 hours. Young children and elderly individuals may be more likely to develop serious reactions. Medical treatment should be sought if the pain is extreme or if there is difficulty in breathing.

Scorpion Stings. Scorpions are usually found in warm areas of the United States, but have been reported as far north as Oregon. Although stings are painful, symptoms are not generally severe. First aid includes cooling the site of the sting and keeping it clean to prevent infection. The Arizona scorpion is potentially dangerous. If pain is severe or lasts more than 4 hours, medical attention is needed.

Travelers should be familiar with the types of venomous creatures found in the areas they visit. Very dangerous snakes, scorpions, and spiders are found in Australia, South America, Africa, and India. Knowing how to identify and avoid potentially dangerous creatures and appropriate first aid could be life saving for the mountaineer traveling in exotic areas.

Tick-Borne Diseases

Ticks are familiar pests throughout the United States. They are common parasites on many animals and are responsible for the transmission of many infectious diseases in humans. New tick-borne diseases have been recognized since 1970, and other diseases have increased dramatically in frequency. Ticks feed on blood obtained by biting people. Chemicals from the ticks rarely act directly as a venom, although small nodules or ulcers may develop at the site of the bite. In very rare instances a condition known as tick paralysis can occur which resolves when the tick is removed from the skin.

Tick-borne diseases are usually caused by the introduction of infectious microorganisms from the tick into the patient. Lyme disease, recognized only since 1975, is the most common disease spread by ticks. It has been reported in almost all states of the United States, and in Europe and Australia, and is seen commonly in the coastal Mid-Atlantic states, the northern West Coast states, Wisconsin, and Minnesota. The initial sign of the disease is usually a distinctive rash surrounding the bite that develops within three to thirty-nine days. It is accompanied by flu-like symptoms of muscular pain, fatigue, and low fevers. If untreated, Lyme disease progresses over several weeks to include problems with the nervous system, heart, and joints. Lyme disease can be treated successfully by antibiotics if it is recognized.

Rocky Mountain Spotted Fever, Colorado Tick Fever, and Relapsing Fever are three of the six or seven major tick-borne diseases found in the United States, although they are much less frequently seen than Lyme disease. Usually there is no sign or symptom associated with the tick bite itself. All of these diseases have incubation periods of two to fourteen days after receiving a bite. Signs of infection may include rashes, fevers, fatigue, or general malaise. If you or a fellow mountaineer experience any of these signs and symptoms after being bitten by a tick, seek medical help. Even if you do not remember being bitten, report your trip and potential exposure to ticks when you see your physician. There is no first aid for tick-borne disease. The wilderness traveler should recognize the importance of tick bites if later illness develops.

Prevention. Tick-borne diseases can be prevented by wearing protective clothing and carefully inspecting all body parts for possible tick attachment when traveling through infested areas. Tight-fitting collars, sleeves, and pant-leg cuffs may help to prevent ticks from crawling onto legs and arms. Spraying *clothing* with insect repellents containing permethrin or DEET (diethyltoluamide—a powerful pesticide) may also prevent attachment of a tick. Do **not** spray permethrin directly on skin. DEET preparations may be applied over other creams on the skin, such as sunscreen, to minimize absorption.

Ticks that spread disease may be very small and their bites not felt. Visual inspection of the skin is important to detect the presence of a small tick. Transmission of the disease-causing agent from the tick usually requires a number of hours of attachment. Prompt removal of ticks may lessen the likelihood of being infected. Ticks should be removed carefully as body parts left in the bite wound can cause problems later.

Remove an unattached tick with tweezers, being careful not to crush or squeeze the body. If the tick is attached, it should be grasped as close as possible to the skin surface using blunt tweezers or fingers protected with tissue. The tick should be pulled out using steady pressure so that body parts are not left in the wound. After the tick is removed, the bite should be cleansed and disinfected.

OTHER MISERIES
Blisters

Blisters are caused by friction from rubbing, which can occur when boots are too large (or too small) or are laced too loosely, or when socks are wrinkled. *Downhill blisters* occur on the toes when the foot slides forward in the boot, and *uphill blisters* are found on the heel.

Prevent Further Injury. Remove the boot and sock at the first sign of a hot spot, and protect any reddened area by covering it with moleskin (or tape or molefoam). Be sure that it extends well beyond the reddened area to reduce friction on the hot spot. If a blister has already formed, keep pressure off of it by applying a doughnut-shaped piece of moleskin or molefoam. Replace damp socks with dry ones.

Prevent Infection. Blisters should not be opened unless absolutely necessary. If it must be done, wash the area with soap and water, and insert a needle (sterilized with a match or rubbing alcohol) at the edge

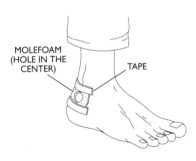

MOLEFOAM
(HOLE IN THE
CENTER)

TAPE

of the blister. Gently press out the fluid and apply a sterile dressing. If the blister has already broken, it should be washed and dressed in the same manner as any open wound. Protect the blister from further friction by placing moleskin on top of the dressing, extending the moleskin well beyond the edges of the blister.

BLISTERS

FIRST AID

Prevent further injury:

Protect a hot spot with moleskin at first indication of pain.

Keep pressure off a blister with a doughnut of molefoam.

Replace damp socks with dry ones.

Prevent infection:

Keep blisters intact.

If you must open a blister, wash it first and then use a sterile needle.

Wash an open blister and cover it with sterile dressing and moleskin to reduce friction.

PREVENTION

Ensure that footwear fits properly and is well broken in.

Wear two layers of socks.

Place tape or moleskin over areas that blister easily.

Use tincture of benzoin to toughen skin.

Retie boots before starting downhill.

Prevention of Blisters. The best prevention of blisters is to wear properly fitting boots, well broken in, with two pairs of socks. Many people put adhesive tape or moleskin over areas that blister easily before hiking. Some people find that benzoin, applied repeatedly over a period of weeks, can toughen the skin. Before starting downhill, boots may need to be retied to prevent the foot from sliding forward.

Dental Emergencies

Toothaches and broken teeth can occur in the wilderness. While severe dental pain is best treated by a dentist, some first aid measures can be taken.

Toothache. Toothaches are caused when the nerve or pulp of a tooth is exposed to air. Aspirin or other pain medication can be taken, and excessively hot, cold, or spicy food should be avoided.

Broken Tooth or Filling. Temporary filling materials, such as Cavit, can be obtained from your dentist and carried in your first aid kit. Rinse the broken surface carefully with clean water. Dry off the surface. Roll the filling material into a small ball and press it into the hole in the tooth.

Avulsed Tooth. A tooth that has been completely removed from its socket can be replaced. If the socket is bleeding, pack it with a small roll of sterile dressing. When bleeding has stopped, gently remove the dressing and rinse the socket with sterile water. Rinse the tooth off with sterile water, handling it only by the crown. Ease the tooth back into the socket with slow, steady pressure. The best outcome occurs if the tooth is replaced within 30 minutes and is cared for by a dentist within a week. If the tooth cannot be replaced, clean it and keep it dry in a sterile dressing. A dentist may be able to replace the tooth at a later time.

Irritation and Infection. Irritation and infections usually result from poor dental hygiene. Salt water rinses (1 teaspoon of table salt to 8 ounces of water) three times a day along with good brushing may relieve irritation. Swelling around the teeth is an indication of infection and is best treated by a dentist. Infections with large amounts of swelling and significant pain are a cause for evacuation to the care of a dentist or physician.

Diarrhea from Contaminated Water

Although a clear mountain stream is likely free of the pollution caused by "civilization," it may well not be free of illness-causing bacteria, viruses, or parasites. The United States Forest Service and National Park Service are currently advising backcountry travelers to treat their water before drinking it to prevent infection with the parasite *Giardia*. Giardiasis is the number-one parasite disease in the United States, and it affects some 10 to 20 percent of the world's population. A trapping study of wild animals in Washington State found *Giardia* in 19 percent of beavers and 43 percent of muskrats. Outbreaks have been reported from New England to California. Not all diarrhea is caused by *Giardia*. Bacteria such as *Shigella, Salmonella,* and *Campylobacter* and viruses such as Poliovirus and Hepatitis A have also been found to cause illness from wilderness water contamination.

If a person becomes infected with *Giardia,* one of three things can happen. *Acute infection* is marked by diarrhea lasting ten days or more, foul-smelling stools and gas, fatigue, and abdominal distention. *Chronic infection* is marked by intermittent episodes of mushy, foul-smelling stools, abdominal pain and distention, gas, loss of appetite, weight loss, and fatigue. *Asymptomatic infection* means no symptoms are noticed by the infected person, but *Giardia* is present in the intestines. These people are carriers of infection, who can unknowingly infect others.

Symptoms of giardiasis, if they develop, occur seven to ten days after infection. Other infections will develop symptoms of diarrhea in much less time. First aid for diarrhea is limited to replacing the lost fluid. A balanced solution of salts and sugar, such as electrolyte replacement drinks, is best. Consultation with a physician may be required for an accurate diagnosis and treatment.

Large outbreaks of *Cryptosporidium* infections from wilderness water sources have been recently recognized. Incubation periods for the disease last from five days to four weeks after exposure. Signs and symptoms include watery diarrhea, cramps, and occasionally low fevers and nausea. The disease is usually limited to five or six days and resolves by itself. In some patients, the illness may be prolonged and involve the respiratory or other body systems. Antibiotics have been effective in treating more serious cases.

Prevention. All water in the wilderness should be treated, even if taken from very clear high altitude sources.

Microorganisms can be transmitted by means other than drinking infected water. Food preparation with dirty hands and other "camp uncleanness" is a more frequent route for the transmission of illness than drinking contaminated water. *Giardia* is frequently transmitted from infant to adult when hands are not sufficiently cleaned after diapering. An outbreak of *Shigella* among rafters on the Colorado River was traced to infected guides who did not carefully wash their hands before preparing food. Since water can be contaminated by infected people as well as infected animals, backcountry sanitation practices are essential. Bury human waste in holes at least 8 inches deep and 200 feet from any water sources, wash your hands with soap and treated water before preparing food, and wash all food preparation eating utensils in treated water. Individuals with diarrhea should not be allowed to prepare food.

Water Treatment. Because the consequences of infection are so unpleasant, the best approach is prevention. You can choose not to drink the water (and carry water from home), or treat it to kill the microorganisms. Water treatment involves either boiling the water, using chemicals, or filtration. All diarrhea-causing microorganisms are killed when water is kept at a temperature of 160°F (70°C) for 30 minutes, or within a few minutes if the temperature is raised to 185°F. Disinfection occurs during the time that water heats from 160°F to boiling: water brought to a boil is safe even at high altitudes. For an extra margin of safety, boil water for 1 minute and leave it covered for several minutes.

Chemical water treatment methods include the use of liquid disinfectants (such as chlorine bleach or povidone-iodine), commercial disinfectant tablets, and the use of iodine crystals in saturated solution. Iodine-based disinfectants have been shown to be more effective than chlorine-based products. When water temperature is 50°F (10°C) the best disinfectant is only 90 percent effective in killing microorganisms after 30 minutes of contact time. With 8 hours of contact, iodine disinfectants are 99.9 percent effective. The clearer the water, the faster the disinfection. Cloudy water should be filtered through a clean cloth before treatment. The taste of treated water can be improved by using less disinfectant and increasing contact time, filtering the water through a charcoal filter *after* treatment, and adding flavoring powders *after* treatment. Follow the directions given by the disinfectant's manufacture. Neither iodine nor chlorine treatments are effective in killing *Cryptosporidium*.

Pregnant women, individuals with known hypersensitivity to iodine, and individuals with a history of thyroid disease themselves in or in their families should talk with their physicians before using iodine-based water treatments. Iodine water treatment should not be used for prolonged periods.

A number of filter devices are available and vary greatly in cost and effectiveness. An effective filtering device must have pores small enough to trap microorganisms and be able to filter a usable amount of water before needing cleaning. *Giardia* can be trapped by a filter with a pore size as large as 5 microns. A filter this size will not trap other smaller parasites, bacteria, or viruses that may also cause disease. A pore size of 2 microns is needed to trap bacteria. Most filters sold for field use will not trap viruses, which are considerably smaller than bacteria. Some newer filters add chemical resins to the water path, which may kill viruses. Filters with very small pores generally need a pump to force water through them. Eventually, the pores will clog with particulate material and need replacing or cleaning. A filtering device that has developed a crack should be discarded.

First Aid. The most important first aid for diarrhea is to make sure that the patient consumes adequate liquid to offset fluid loss and prevent dehydration. Treated water or electrolyte replacement fluids may be used. One replacement fluid can be made by combining 1 teaspoon salt, 3 tablespoons sugar, and 1 liter of treated water. A good replacement fluid is treated water mixed with starch-based products, such CeraLyte. Although expensive, these products enhance absorption of fluid and electrolytes.

DIARRHEA FROM CONTAMINATED WATER

PREVENTION

Treat all water.

Bury human waste in holes at least 8 inches deep and 200 feet from any water sources.

Wash your hands with soap and treated water before preparing food.

Wash all eating utensils in treated water.

Do **not** allow individuals with diarrhea to prepare food.

WATER TREATMENT

Use one of the following methods:

Boil water for 1 minute and leave it covered for several minutes.

Use chemical water treatment products. (Not all organisms will be killed.)

Use filter devices. (Not all organisms may be captured or killed.)

FIRST AID

Provide adequate liquid to offset fluid loss and prevent dehydration.

If diarrhea persists, give two tablets of bismuth subsalicylate every 30 minutes for eight doses.

Seek medical care if diarrhea persists for more than a week or symptoms are severe.

Bismuth subsalicylate (Pepto-Bismol) can be given. Take two tablets every half hour, but do not exceed eight doses (sixteen tablets) within a 24-hour period. Individuals allergic to aspirin or pregnant women should not take bismuth subsalicylate.

Seek medical care if you have three or more loose stools in an 8-hour period, the diarrhea persists for several days (more than one week), or if other severe signs and symptoms (blood in the stools, fever, nausea, severe cramps) are present.

Fainting

Fainting is caused by a temporary lessening of blood flow to the brain, generally from blood pooling in the legs. It can result from a wide variety of processes, including prolonged standing, especially in the heat; sudden standing after resting; or less often, from fright (such as upon encountering Sasquatch). Unconsciousness that lasts for more than 3 minutes is not considered fainting. First aid for fainting consists of positioning the patient flat, with lower legs raised. First aid for heat illness may also be indicated.

Headache

Headache in the mountains can result from dehydration, eye strain from inadequate protection from the sun, or tension in the neck muscles. It can also result from lack of sleep or be related to drinking alcohol (a habit not unknown to mountaineers). Less often, it is an early sign of a more serious problem, such as heat exhaustion or Acute Mountain Sickness. In any case of headache, the source of the trouble should be sought and first aid given as appropriate. Aspirin may relieve the immediate pain.

Infectious Disease from Wild Animals

A number of significant diseases can be transmitted from wild animals to humans in a wilderness setting. Rabies is found in bats, raccoons, and skunks and usually is transmitted by the bite of an infected animal. It can also be transmitted by inhalation of aerosols containing the virus in humid bat-infested caves. Plague has been reported in ground squirrels and rodents and tularemia is found in rabbits. These diseases are transmitted by bites from infected animals, from skinning or handling the tissues of infected animals, eating improperly cooked infected meat, or inhaling dust particles from dried feces. Hantavirus is found in deer mice and other rodents and is transmitted by inhaling dust from excreta or disturbing rodent nests. Contact local authorities to inquire about outbreaks of animal-transmitted diseases.

The best advice for prevention of these diseases is to avoid contact with infected animals. Set up camp away from animal burrows and possible rodent shelters such as woodpiles. Avoid cabins, other buildings, or woodpiles that have been infested with rodents. Do not sleep on the bare ground: use tents with floors. Keep food and water stored in animal-proof containers. Be aware of any local warnings about infected wild animals, and stay out of posted areas. If bitten, immediately and aggressively clean the wound and seek professional help. If possible without further injury to you or the patient, capture the animal for testing by public health personnel.

Lightning Injuries

While injuries due to lightning are rare, when they occur they can be significant. The most common cause of death from lightning is cardiopulmonary arrest. The heart may begin to beat on its own, but the respiratory arrest may continue for a much longer time. It is essential that rescue breathing or CPR, as appropriate, is begun immediately when a lightning victim is found without respiration or heartbeat. The next most serious and common injury is to the central nervous system, followed by burns to the skin and internal organs caused by the passage of electricity through the body (see page 99). Any survivor of a lightning strike should be evacuated to a medical facility.

Prevention of lightning injuries during an electrical storm includes avoiding open areas and single rocks or trees that are the tallest objects in an open area; avoiding metal objects; seeking shelter in a dry cave or a group of trees or rocks; squatting on a foam pad or coil of rope; and spreading out but staying in visual contact with other party members.

FIRST AID FOR INFANTS AND CHILDREN

Children are different from adults in a number of ways that affect the first aid given to them. One obvious difference is that children are smaller than adults. Consequently, children will have more serious reactions to bites and stings than adults, even when the amount of venom injected is the same. Similarly, children are more likely to suffer toxic reactions to agents such as insect repellents and sunscreens. Children gain and lose heat faster than adults, making them more susceptible to environmental illnesses. They are at greater risk for hypothermia, problems with overheating, and sunburn. They become dehydrated more quickly as well.

Once children become ill, the first aid care for them is the same as for adults: hypothermic children need to be taken out of the cold and damp, and a snake-bitten child needs to be taken to a medical facility. The most important concept in dealing with first aid for infants and children is that parents need to be very active in prevention of injury and illness and vigilant in observing their children for signs of illness. Young children must be protected from heat, cold, and the sun. Campsites need to be safe for young children, away from cliffs, lakes, and streams. Access to sharp-edged tools must be restricted and open fires carefully controlled. Routes need to be chosen to suit the stamina and abilities of children. Young children are less able to express themselves and inform parents of their physical conditions. Use physical signs and changes in behavior as guides to identifying illness in children. What might seem to be a minor event for an adult may require an immediate evacuation for a child.

A few specific recommendations for dealing with children and infants' first aid and illness prevention needs can be made.

- Provide adequate food and water for children. As children are finicky eaters, foods to be eaten on a trip should be tested at home for palatability.
- Test sunscreens on a small patch of the child's skin for an allergic reaction before using it on a trip.
- Do not overtire children. Children's size, energy, and personality limit the distances they are able to walk or hike. Children under two years of age need to be carried. A four-year-old may be able to walk up to 2 miles in one day with very frequent stops. A seven-year-old can hike up to about 3 hours a day and cover 4 miles. The nine-year-old can cover 7 miles and hike for a full day, and if over 4 feet tall, will be able to carry a small frame pack. A twelve-year-old will hike a full day at a moderate pace and cover 10 miles.
- Do not allow insect repellents containing permethrin to touch a child's skin. Spray them only on clothing. Use repellents with DEET in low concentrations, preferably no more than 10 percent. Insect repellents that contain DEET may be applied over other creams, such as sunscreen, to minimize absorption into the skin. Keep all repellents out of the reach of children as they may be toxic.
- Children young enough to be in diapers should be wetting them at least once every 8 hours. If not, the child is probably dehydrated. Diarrhea can also quickly lead to dehydration. Sweetened solutions are inappropriate for rehydration. A mixture of 1 teaspoon of table salt and 1 cup of rice cereal in a quart of water is an excellent rehydration solution. Give 2 to 3 ounces of fluid for every 2.2 pounds of the child's weight every 4 hours until signs of dehydration have resolved. Any unused solution must be discarded after 12 hours.
- Toileting for young children can be a source of infection. Make sure there are adequate diapers and cleansing supplies for the trip. Extra clothing and underwear may be helpful in case of accidents. Insist that children AND adults wash their hands after using the toilet.
- Check with your child's physician before administering any medication to a child, including any over-the-counter drug. If

your child is susceptible to infections, ask your child's physician for antibiotics in advance and indications for their use.

- Use acetaminophen for fever reduction or pain relief. Avoid aspirin or other salicylate medications. Follow your physician's recommendation for dosage.
- Keep travel plans simple and flexible. Always have plans for evacuation in mind. Never let your travel plans or interests prevent you from detecting an illness in your child or making a decision to cut a trip short.
- Pulse and respiratory rates are higher in children and infants. The pulse of an infant is taken on the inside surface of the upper arm at the brachial artery. Some infants and young children will have body temperatures slightly higher than adults, 99° to 101°F.

PULSE AND RESPIRATORY RATES OF CHILDREN

AGE	HEARTBEATS PER MINUTE	BREATHS PER MINUTE
12 to 15 years	55 to 115	15 to 21
5 to 7 years	70 to 130	15 to 26
1 to 2 years	90 to 150	17 to 33
2 to 5 months	100 to 180	28 to 52

Rescue Breathing and Clearing an Obstructed Airway in Infants and Young Children

Rescue breathing and airway management skills for a child older than eight years are the same as those for adults, as discussed in Chapter 2 (see page 37). The skills are the same for younger children with the following exceptions:

- In infants and children less than eight years old, rescue breaths should be given at a rate of one every 3 seconds, and the volume should be only enough to raise the chest. Also, the head does not need to be tilted as far back as an adult in order to open the airway. Tilt the head only far enough to allow air to enter.
- Clearing an obstructed airway in a conscious child uses abdominal thrusts until the child begins to breathe. To perform abdominal thrusts, place the thumb side of your fist just above the child's navel. Grab your fist with your other hand and give

quick, upward thrusts. You may need to kneel behind the child.

INFANTS

- The method for clearing an obstructed airway in an unconscious child one year or older includes chest compressions about 1½ inches deep done with one hand. Attempt to give two breaths. If air does not go in, reposition the child's head and try two breaths again. If air still does not go in, give five chest compressions and conduct a visual check for foreign objects in the mouth. Give one rescue breath. If air

CHILDREN

does not go in, repeat the cycle of chest compressions and breath until the object has been cleared. These skills for children are best practiced in a CPR course.
- Clearing an obstructed airway in an infant includes a series of back blows and chest thrusts best learned in an infant CPR class.

Step 6: Plan What to Do

Previous sections have focused on identifying types of injuries and describing first aid care. Except for meeting the urgent first aid needs of impaired breathing and severe bleeding, there is no need to treat an injury as soon as it is found. It is better to stop and plan carefully what will be done and in what order. Planning can prevent moving the injured person unnecessarily or getting halfway through a treatment and having to undo it so that another part of the treatment can be done. The plan extends beyond the patient's immediate first aid needs to include deciding on means of evacuation and roles party members will play. Although the final plan is the leader's responsibility, information should be obtained from other party members. The leader should discuss with party members specific suggestions for first aid needs of the patients and the utilization of party resources as well as plans for any patient movement.

DECIDING TO END A TRIP

One of the first decisions to be made is whether to postpone further travel or to end a trip. In many instances it will be clear that a patient cannot continue traveling and the trip must end. In other instances, many party members may be anxious to continue and the need to end the trip will not be clear. A trip should be postponed or ended if any of the following conditions are present in a patient:

- The patient's condition is deteriorating
- Pain or injury that prevents travel, or a medical condition that compromises the ability to travel
- Serious high altitude illness
- Infections that persist for more than 24 hours

- Unexplained passage of blood
- Severe chest pain
- Psychological changes that impair the safety of the patient

ESTABLISH PRIORITIES

When planning care, a priority list of treatment needs should be established. Answering the following questions can help in determining the order of first aid activities:

- *Are some patients more seriously injured than others?* Party resources may need to be focused on the most seriously injured in order that they may survive. Less seriously injured patients may get only a small part of the available help because they can survive with less assistance. Alternatively, if the needs of one patient are beyond the capacity of the party, then the party's resources should be directed toward caring for patients with injuries where they have a chance of success.
- *Which injuries will cause the most harm if left unattended?* A broken leg may be painful, but it is not as hazardous to the patient's survival as hypothermia left untreated.
- *Can treatment of one problem assist in the treatment of another?* For example, when moving onto insulation, the patient can also be placed onto the ties needed for splinting.

Making a priority list will help ensure that all treatment needs are met and that equipment and party members are used to the best advantage.

PLANNING FOR FIRST AID

Once priorities for patient care have been determined, plans for specific treatments to be undertaken need to be discussed. Personnel, equipment, and supplies needed to carry out the treatments should be identified. Some treatments may require that a rescuer is temporarily moved from one patient to another, until the treatment is completed. The equipment and supplies of the rescuers and the injured patients should be included in the plan. Resources that are needed to either stay in place until help arrives or that are required during a self-evacuation of the party must be identified.

If a patient is to be moved, then the sequence of treatments and the expected place where the patient will stay until evacuation is attempted should be carefully thought out so that movement is minimized. Tents or other shelters should be prepared in advance of the movement, and every rescuer should have a clear understanding of how the move is to be accomplished. If possible, the party should rehearse a movement in advance of attempting it with the patient.

PATIENT MOVEMENT: SHORT-DISTANCE TRANSFER

Short-distance transfer may be needed to move a patient off the snow, out of the rain, or into a tent. Transferring a patient to another location can improve comfort. More important, moving the patient may be essential to first aid treatment and the patient's well-being. For the seriously injured patient, the **least** amount of movement is best. More harm can be done through improper transfer than through any other measure associated with first aid. Transfer of a patient should be done only when absolutely necessary and with a great deal of care and forethought. Transfer methods are easily learned, but must be practiced before being used on a patient. The ability to use movement techniques correctly is of particular concern in the mountains because of the possibility of fall-related injuries to the back, head, and neck. All movement should take place only after respiration and circulation have been stabilized, and the initial pain and fear of injury has subsided. Movement, except for emergency rescue, occurs in Step 7.

In moving a patient, the following procedures must be observed:
- Plan moves so that the patient must be moved only once.
- Prepare any insulating materials or shelter before the patient is moved.
- The transfer process should be rehearsed carefully, using a rescuer as practice subject. Directions for the transfer should be practiced.
- The rescuer supporting the head is the leader of the transfer. Other rescuers should precisely follow the movement and direction of the leader.
- Protection of the patient's entire body must be assured during the move.
- The body of a patient with a suspected neck or back injury should be kept in a straight line, from the top of the head down the spine and through the buttocks.
- A "scout," a rescuer not holding onto the patient, may be appointed to help the rescuers avoid obstacles and travel over rough terrain.

Directions for several patient moves follow.

Two-Handed Seat Carry—Two Rescuers
1. Preparation. The move has been included in the plan for first aid. Insulation materials, tents, etc. are ready, path of movement has been cleared, and the safety of the rescuers considered.
2. Rescuers assume a position behind the patient facing each other.

3. If the patient is sitting on the ground, the rescuers kneel down on the knee closest to the patient. The rescuer's arm closest to the patient is placed across the patient's back and into the patient's far armpit. The other hand is placed from the front of the patient into the closest armpit.

4. The rescuers stand at the same time, bringing the patient to a vertical position.

5. The patient's arms are placed around the rescuers' necks. The rescuers' arms closest to the patient support the patient's back. The rescuers may interlock their arms to form a backrest.

6. The rescuers grasp each other's arms at the wrists to form a seat for the patient.

7. Crouch so that the patient may sit down on the seat.

8. Once the patient is securely seated, stand.

Transfer of a Patient with a Suspected Back or Neck Injury

A patient with a suspected back or neck injury should be evacuated on a rigid backboard or stretcher. A rigid stretcher or board cannot be made from the materials typically at hand in a mountaineering situation, and its use requires training. Until a rigid stretcher can be brought to the scene of the accident, it is better to leave the patient as found, putting a shelter up around the patient rather than attempting to move the patient into shelter.

If the patient must be moved to allow placement of insulation between the patient and the ground, or must be transferred a short distance, the following techniques may be used. At all times during the movement, the patient's head and back must be kept in straight alignment. Once the move has ended, the head must be supported by a rescuer until it is secured with sandbags. The following techniques can be modified for use with patients found in positions other than lying flat on their backs.

Log-Roll of a Patient onto Insulation: Lying on the Back
  1. Preparation. The move has been included in the plan for first aid. Insulation materials, sandbags, etc. are ready. Four rescuers are needed.
  2. The leader of the move assumes a position directly behind the patient's head. The rescuer's hands are positioned with fingers placed supporting the back of the head and the jaw, typically with the palms of the hands covering the ears. This may be modified due to the size of the rescuer's hands compared to the patient's head or the position of the patient. The intent is to prevent motion of the patient's head relative to the rest of the body.
  3. If necessary, the patient's head and neck may be moved gently and slowly to form a straight line with the spine. If there is **any** resistance to the movement, or the patient experiences **any** pain, the movement must **stop immediately**, and the head and neck be left in their present position.
  4. The other rescuers assume positions on one side of the patient, kneeling on both knees. One rescuer is placed near the shoulders, the second at the hips, and a third at the knees.
  5. The insulation material is placed on the far side of the patient, ready to move under the patient. The pad must be long enough to provide insulation under the head, trunk, buttocks, and upper legs of the patient. Preferably, the pad should extend from the top of the head to the heels. The edge of the material next to the patient may

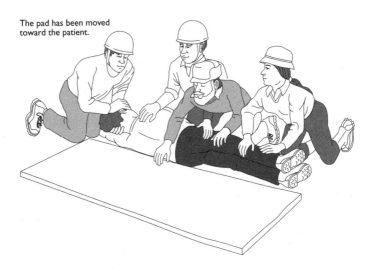

The pad has been moved toward the patient.

be rolled under itself, so that after the patient has been placed on the insulation the rolled edge may be gently unrolled.

6. The patient's arm on the same side as the rescuers is lifted up and out of the way of the roll, while the patient's shoulder is supported by the rescuer's other arm to reduce movement of the patient's spine.

7. The rescuer at the shoulders secures the patient's opposite arm putting the patient's hand in a pocket or waistband.

8. The rescuer at the shoulder places one hand at the patient's far shoulder and the second at the hips. The rescuer at the hips places one hand at the top of the hips (in between the first rescuer's hands) and the second hand at mid-thigh. The third rescuer places one hand at the knees and the other hand at the ankles.

9. The leader calls "Prepare to roll," and when all are ready, "Roll." The patient is slowly rolled toward the rescuers' knees. The patient is moved as a unit, with the leader setting the pace. The patient's head, neck, and spine are kept in a straight line. The rescuer at the hips moves the insulation next to the patient.

10. The leader calls "Prepare to lower," and when all are ready, "Lower": the patient is rolled onto the material.

11. The rescuer at the patient's head remains in place until the head is secured with sandbags.

Five-Person-Carry for Short-Distance Transfer

1. Preparation. The move has been included in the plan for first aid. Insulation materials, tents, etc. are ready, the path of movement

has been cleared, and the safety of the rescuers considered.

2. The leader of the move assumes a position directly behind the patient's head. Hands are placed on either side of the head as in Step 1 of the log-roll.

3. If necessary, the patient's head and neck may be moved gently and slowly to form a straight line with the spine. If there is **any** resistance to the movement, or the patient experiences **any** pain, the movement must **stop immediately**, and the head and neck be left in their present position.

4. Other rescuers assume positions on both sides of the patient at the shoulders, waist, hips, and lower legs. Rescuers at the shoulders and the hips are on the same side of the patient, the rescuers at the waist and lower legs are on the opposite side of the patient. All rescuers kneel on the knee closest to the patient's head.

5. The patient's arms are secured by gently tying them at the wrist or placing the hands in the patient's waistband.

6. The rescuer at the shoulders gently moves one hand under the top of the shoulders (also supporting the lower portion of the neck), and the other hand at the lowest edge of the patient's ribs. The rescuer at the waist places one hand under the ribs (just above the first rescuer's hand) and the other hand just below the patient's waist. The rescuer at the hips places one hand under the patient's waist and the other hand at mid-thigh. The rescuer at the lower legs places one hand just under the knees and the other hand

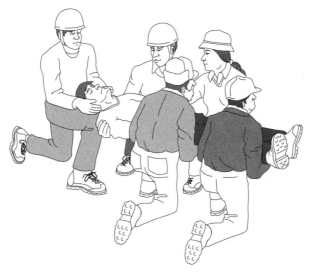

under the lower legs. One hand of the rescuer at the waist will be between the hands of the rescuer at the shoulder, and the other hand will be between the hands of the rescuer at the hips.

7. The leader calls "Prepare to lift to knees," and when all are ready, "Lift." At the second call, the patient is slowly lifted onto the rescuers' knees. The patient is moved as a unit, with the leader setting the pace.

8. Rescuers' hands are slid further underneath the patient. The bend of the rescuers' arms should be directly next to the patient; the rescuers' upper arms should be in contact with the side of the patient's body. The rescuers at the shoulder, waist, and hips may grasp the arms of the opposite rescuers.

9. The leader calls "Prepare to stand," and when all are ready, "Stand." At the second call, the rescuers stand erect. Any further motion is directed by the leader. When walking, rescuers shuffle their feet side to side. Do not cross over legs to take steps.

Lowering the patient is the reverse of the procedure.

10. The leader calls "Prepare to lower to knees," and when all are ready, "Lower." The patient is slowly lowered onto the rescuers' knees. The rescuers kneel on the knee closest to the patient's head on the ground.

11. The rescuers move their arms to the position described in Step 6. The leader calls "Prepare to lower to ground," and when all are ready, "Lower," and the rescuers lower the patient to the ground.

The exact position of the rescuers' hands from shoulders to hips will vary with the size of the patient and the rescuers. The intent is to provide good support for the shoulders, back, and hips.

DECIDING TO EVACUATE

After establishing a priority list for meeting the first aid needs of the patients, the leader must consider what needs to be done to keep the party safe and ensure that the injured get to appropriate treatment. One of the most difficult questions to be answered is how the injured person will get to outside help. Will the party self-evacuate or request outside help? Several conditions must be considered in making this decision:

- *What is the extent of the patient's injuries?* A minor injury may slow the party down, but given enough time the patient will be able to walk out. Several relatively minor injuries or a severe injury may require more help than the party can provide.
- *What is the terrain that must be crossed?* A patient with a broken

wrist may be able to walk down a trail easily but have difficulty scrambling across a boulder field.

- *What is the weather?* Walking across an alpine slope in bright sunshine is much easier than trying to cross the same slope in wind, rain, and fog.
- *How far is it to the trailhead?* An injured patient may be able to walk a mile or two, but not five or ten.
- *What is the party strength?* Party strength includes the number of people, their condition, experience, and the equipment they have to use as well as the rescue skills and knowledge that the members possess. A tired, psychologically distraught, or inexperienced party may be unable to accomplish a self-evacuation of even a minor injury.
- *What equipment is available?* Assemble all equipment, including the patient's, in one place and take an inventory. Determine what is available, and what additional equipment should be brought in by a rescue party. Plan to use the patient's equipment first.
- *How much outside help is available? How long will it take to reach the accident scene?* In the mountains, outside help is usually 6 to 24 hours away. Even a slowly moving patient may be able to get out to help faster than help can arrive.

The decision may not be a simple choice of self-evacuation versus requesting outside help but a combination of the two types of evacuation. A party may move the patient a short distance to a safer or more comfortable location. They may self-evacuate to the point at which technical rescue techniques beyond the party's capacity are required. The party may move slowly down the trail toward the rescuers, thereby saving time.

ISSUES TO CONSIDER IN EVACUATION PLANS

What is the extent of the patient's injuries?
What is the terrain that must be crossed?
What is the weather?
How far is it to the trailhead?
What is the party strength?
What equipment is available?
How much outside help is available; how long will it take to reach the accident scene?

Self-Evacuation

Most parties are not sufficiently strong or well equipped to safely evacuate a seriously injured patient. A minimum of eight rescuers is needed to handle a patient in a litter at any one time, and carriers should be rotated off duty every 15 to 20 minutes. Travel over off-trail terrain may require sixty or more rescuers for a trip of any distance more than a few hundred feet. Patients with relatively minor injuries can, with patience and care, be safely evacuated even by a small party. The leader, when deciding if self-evacuation is possible, must consider the extent of the injuries, the type of terrain to be covered, and the strength of other party members. The leader must also consider what will happen if the party starts to self-evacuate and is unable to continue. Will there be a safe place to stop? Several criteria must be met for a successful self-evacuation.

The patient must be willing to help and must understand how to aid in the self-evacuation. All injuries must be treated prior to starting out. One person should accompany the patient at all times. He or she can provide both encouragement and physical assistance when needed. This individual will also need to monitor the patient's condition and the safety of the evacuation procedures.

Each section of the route should be checked prior to attempting to navigate it with the patient. The other party members will have to travel the route at least two or even three times. Ways around obstacles need to be found prior to the arrival of the patient so that he or she does not have to backtrack or cross unnecessarily difficult areas. An apparently quicker more direct route might require the use of more balance or climbing techniques than the patient is capable of doing. A slight uphill section, barely noticed under normal conditions, may be an insurmountable barrier to the injured patient.

In summary, Step 6 of the Seven Steps is to plan for activities needed to ensure a successful response.

Step 7: Carry Out the Plan

After a thorough examination of the entire accident situation and development of a plan, the party is ready to carry out its plan. The leader needs to ensure that all aspects of the first aid care are done. Minor injuries should not be overlooked in the press of caring for major injuries. If help is to be sought, adequate information must be collected into a report and rescuers must be prepared to reach the trailhead. If a helicopter rescue is possible, a landing site must be prepared.

Attention must also be given to how well the plan is working. Is the patient's condition improving or getting worse? Is the party getting weaker, are party members becoming hypothermic? Is the party getting stronger and more confident as they realize they can handle the situation? Are there changes in terrain or weather that make the plan unworkable or inadequate? Constant evaluation of the plan must be made and changes made as needed.

SENDING OUT FOR HELP

How quickly help will arrive, and how adequate it will be, depends on the kind of information sent out and the messenger's ability to deliver that information. Whenever possible, at least two people should be sent for help. **The party members should not be sent until adequate information about the patient is available, the accident site is under control, and it is certain that their help will not be needed.** The people sent should be strong members of the party not only in terms of physical strength but also in terms of experience and judgment. They must be able to get themselves out safely and deliver their message clearly and completely to the appropriate authorities. The messengers may also be asked to serve as guides back to the accident site.

The messengers should take the following information:

- Name, age, address, and phone number of patient; people to be notified, and their relationships to the patient
- Where, when, and how the accident occurred
- The number of people injured or ill, and the nature and seriousness of the injuries
- The first aid administered and the condition of the patient, including pulse, respiration, and other vital signs from the initial exam and at the time the messengers left the party
- How many people are still at the scene, what is their condition and level of experience
- What equipment is still at the scene, including both first aid supplies and general equipment
- A list of needed equipment—a rigid stretcher, food, water, shelter, etc.
- The party's **exact location,** and whether they will wait at the scene or move to safer or more readily accessible ground
- Distance from the road and type of terrain: glacier, rock, or trail; be sure to include special information about local conditions, for example: "The last half mile of trail is covered with hard snow and is very steep"
- Local weather conditions, for example: is the accident site above the clouds, or is it very cloudy or windy
- Method of evacuation necessary: carrying by rigid stretcher, sliding on snow, or lowering down steep cliffs
- The names and addresses of all members in the party and whom to notify

Since it is impossible to remember all the information required, a written report, such as the first aid report form, must be carried out. The messengers will also need car keys and coins for the telephone.

The individuals going for help should clearly mark the route. Brightly colored plastic surveyor's tape may be used. Any turn of the route or place where it leaves the trail should be especially well marked. The route and the exact location of the accident should be marked on a topographic map and brought out by the messengers.

Once the messengers reach a telephone, the proper agency must be notified of the accident. Which agency has jurisdiction depends on the location of the accident. In national parks the messengers should contact a ranger. Outside of national parks, the responsible agency for rescues is usually the sheriff or state police department, and in Canada it is the Royal Canadian Mounted Police. If 911 is dialed, the party member must stay on the phone until connected to a representative of the appropriate agency to undertake the rescue. Even when the proper agency has been contacted, the person on the telephone may not be familiar with rescue procedures or be uncertain if the accident is within their jurisdiction. The messengers must be persistent and patient in communicating the accident information to ensure that it does reach the person responsible for the agency's rescue response. The messengers should remain at the telephone and be available if further information is needed. Rescue leaders may want to speak with the messengers, or they may even ask the messengers to return with them to the accident site.

HANDHELD RADIOS AND CELLULAR PHONES
With their increasing availability and miniaturization, handheld radios and cellular phones are finding their way into the packs of hikers and climbers. Stories are told of helicopter rescues on major mountain peaks being completed in a few hours when help was summoned with a cell phone. These devices can be helpful in evacuation situations, but there are some limitations to their use. Most handheld devices are limited in ability to transmit messages outside of urban areas. If you cannot see your target or a repeater tower (which will pick up your signal and transmit it forward) is not nearby, you will be unable to talk with it.

Handheld Citizen Band radios are lightweight, relatively inexpensive, and virtually free from licenses or regulations. They are somewhat limited in range by their power source, and their radio frequencies are usually not monitored by forest service officials or search-and-rescue volunteers. Your best bet of being heard is if a metropolitan area is in sight, or if you know the radio channel used by loggers and truckers in the area.

Another alternative is a two-meter handheld radio. Use of a ham radio requires the operator to pass a test of theory and operation and obtain a license. Institutions or clubs that maintain repeater stations will usually allow occasional free use of their repeaters. Repeater frequency guidebooks with access information are available. Membership in amateur radio clubs may bring additional benefits such as the ability to use the radio to make direct phone calls.

Cell phones are already in the hands of many people. They are small and lightweight but are limited by their dependence on relay stations. Relay stations are not frequently found in the backcountry but are being installed in popular but remote recreation areas such as ski areas or national parks. A call to the Emergency Medical System (911) may get you connected to a service that is unused to handling mountain rescues, or an urban system that is not in the county from which you are calling. Calling directly to the local sheriff's office, the National Park Service, or a search-and-rescue organization might result in a more efficient rescue response. If you contact 911, ask to be connected to the sheriff's office of the county in which the accident has occurred and stay on the line until it is clear that you have contacted someone knowledgeable about rescue activities.

Handheld radios and phones may aid in summoning help to an accident scene, but they do mean additional weight in the pack and are limited by their range and the availability of repeater or relay stations.

HELICOPTER RESCUE

The helicopter has revolutionized mountain rescue. It has quickly evacuated injured from cliffs and glaciers directly to hospitals when it would have taken days of rough, exhausting travel by ground. The helicopter is not, however, the "magic machine" some people think it to be. The weather may be such that a helicopter cannot respond. It may be clear where you are but fogged in at the takeoff point. There may not be any helicopter available, or you may be too far from its base or the closest fuel supply. Operations in the mountains are also very hazardous to both the pilot and the machine, and the costs of helicopter operations are very high. Never assume that a helicopter can come to your rescue.

Choose a Landing Site. When requesting outside help, the party should choose a possible helicopter landing site and send out information on that site. The landing site should ideally be approachable from all sides for landings and takeoffs—a flat-topped ridge, for example. If a ridge is not close by, then choose a relatively flat area. The higher the elevation, the less load a helicopter can carry and the more important a gradual takeoff becomes. A vertical takeoff is very demanding on the aircraft even at sea level and may actually be impossible in the mountains.

Prepare the Landing Site. The landing site should be prepared prior to the arrival of the helicopter. The landing site should be made as level as possible. Mark the landing area with colored tape or other brightly colored objects. **Securely anchor all objects** in the immediate area. Wind from the rotor can approach 60 to 120 miles per hour. Loose materials, such as ground cloths, sleeping bags, or clothing, can easily be blown upward into the rotor blades and cause serious prob-

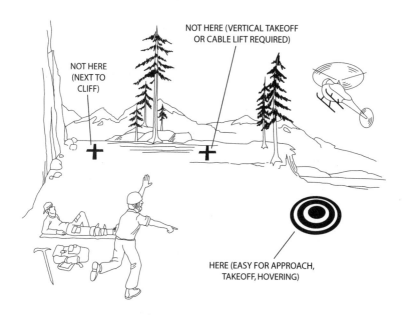

NOT HERE (VERTICAL TAKEOFF OR CABLE LIFT REQUIRED)

NOT HERE (NEXT TO CLIFF)

HERE (EASY FOR APPROACH, TAKEOFF, HOVERING)

lems. If the landing site is on soft snow, pack the site as much as possible to prevent blowing snow that could obstruct the pilot's vision.

Prepare the Patient. Prior to the arrival of the helicopter, the patient should be prepared for helicopter travel. Helicopters have limited fuel and cannot wait around very long while the patient is readied. Explain to the patient what you are doing and that when the helicopter arrives there will be a lot of noise and wind. Tie the patient's hands together if he or she is unconscious or semiconscious. Eye, ear, and head protection should be put on the patient. Any gear going with the patient should be placed in packs or stuff sacks. Be sure not to send out equipment such as ropes or clothing that may be needed later. Make sure that there are no loose straps or clothing. Attach in an obvious but very secure place the first aid record of the patient's injuries and first aid treatment given.

Approach and Landing. Brightly colored objects and arm-waving people are barely visible from the air. Consequently, when the helicopter approaches the area a signal with a smoke flare or a mirror can greatly speed up the pilot's locating the landing site. Once the helicopter is close, indicate wind direction using streamers of plastic surveyor's tape or a pair of rain pants. If none of these is available, a party member can stand with arms extended toward the landing site, which indicates "Land here, my back is to the wind."

The following basic rules must be followed when the helicopter arrives:

- All people in the landing area should have eye protection and hard hats should be worn, if available. Dirt and other materials will be blown about the area when the helicopter lands.
- If the helicopter lowers a cable with a message, radio, or stretcher, allow it to touch ground first to dissipate static electricity.
- Stay at least 75 feet away from the helicopter when it is landing. **Approach the helicopter only after signaled to by the pilot or crew chief.**
- **Always** approach or leave the helicopter from the front so the pilot can see you at all times. **Never** go around the back of the helicopter, because the rear rotor blades are almost invisible and very dangerous.
- Always approach or leave the helicopter from the downhill side.
- Keep your head low, since the slower the rotor is moving the lower the blades will dip.
- Always follow the directions of the pilot or crew.

PATIENT MONITORING

Once Step 7 has started, one person should be assigned to continue monitoring and recording the patient's condition. Recording the patient's vital signs and treatment given is essential in determining how well the plan is being carried out and how well the treatment is working. Vital signs, as important indicators of the patient's well-being, need to be taken at regular intervals by the monitor.

The monitor is someone who stays with the patient constantly, who provides ever-present contact. Every patient in the mountaineering setting will be anxious about what is happening. It is the function of the monitor to stay by the side of the patient to provide reassurance and listen to his or her concerns. It is necessary to have the task of patient monitor assigned to one individual, because other members of the party may be doing something else, such as caring for another patient or having a conference about setting priorities. Monitoring the patient is continued until the patient's care is assumed by someone skilled at a more advanced level.

ALTERING THE PLAN

Whatever the plan of action, both the leader and other party members will have to work together to carry out the plan successfully. The party will need to monitor the patient's condition and response to treatment. The party must not only work hard to carry out the plan but also be willing to make changes if the plan is not working or if conditions change. Above all, you must keep open minds and think about what is needed and the alternatives that are available to take care of those needs.

Even with the best care that can be given, the injuries the patient has sustained may result in death. The death of a patient can be very frightening to first aiders, causing them to feel insecure or afraid for their own lives. Some may feel guilt or remorse for their inability to save the patient's life. If the patient dies, the leader will need to alter the focus from treating the patient to caring for party members. Directing each individual to constructive tasks of rescuing and caring for each other may be the most important task of the leader in the event of a death.

In summary, Step 7 of the Seven Steps is to carry out and monitor the results of first aid activities.

CONCLUSION

An accident scene is an extremely confused place. It is very difficult to sort through the things that can be done, to identify those which must be done, and then to accomplish them in proper order. Following the Seven Steps for First Aid Response can help guide the party members through the numerous tasks involved in performing first aid in a mountaineering environment. Like rock climbing or skiing, it *does* take practice to become proficient. First aid courses with practical instruction in responding to mountaineering accidents are important components of training.

Tremendous problems exist in the event of an accident in the backcountry far from medical care. Awareness of these problems may lead to a better sense of judgment and stimulate a conscientious effort to prevent injuries. Prevention includes knowing the causes of injuries and illness, planning one's own activities, and helping others to be aware of their own responsibilities for injury prevention. All who venture into the mountains have a responsibility to possess a working knowledge of how to respond to an accident situation. They have an even greater responsibility to help prevent avoidable injuries in the out-of-doors.

Additional Reading

Two major technical resources for wilderness medicine, written for physicians and other medical personnel:

Auerbach, P. S., ed. *Wilderness Medicine: Management of Wilderness and Environmental Emergencies,* 4th Edition. St. Louis, MO: Mosby, 2001.

Forgey, W. W., ed. *Wilderness Medical Society Practice Guidelines for Wilderness Emergency Care,* 2nd Edition. Guilford, CT: Globe Pequot Press, 2001.

Basic first aid guides, urban and wilderness:

American National Red Cross. *Community First Aid and Safety.* San Bruno, CA: StayWell, 2002.

American National Red Cross. *Emergency Response.* San Bruno, CA: StayWell, 2001.

Schimelpfenig, T., and L. Lindsey. *NOLS Wilderness First Aid,* 3rd Edition. Mechanicsburg, PA: Stackpole Books, 2000.

Other publications of interest to mountaineers:

Accidents in North American Mountaineering. Golden, CO: American Alpine Club, Inc., (published yearly).

Auerbach, P. S., H. J. Donner, and E. A. Weiss. *Field Guide to Wilderness Medicine.* Philadelphia: Mosby, 2003.

Bezruchka, S. *Altitude Illness: Prevention and Treatment.* Seattle: The Mountaineers Books, 1994.

Wilkerson, J. A., ed. *Hypothermia, Frostbite, and Other Cold Injuries.* Seattle: The Mountaineers Books, 1993.

Wilkerson, J. A., ed. *Medicine for Mountaineering and Other Wilderness Activities,* 5th Edition. Seattle: The Mountaineers Books, 2001.

Index

START HERE	FINDINGS	FIRST
Airway, Breathing, Circulation		
SCAN FOR URGENT INJURIES (Chest Wounds, Severe Bleeding)		
WHAT HAPPENED WHERE IT HURTS ALLERGIES, MEDICAL CONDITIONS		
PULSE & RESPIRATIONS ⎯⎯ PULSE ⎯⎯ RESPIRATIONS		
SKIN: Color Temperature Moistness		
PUPILS: Regular in size Equally reactive		
STATE OF CONSCIOUSNESS:		
PAIN (Location)		
HEAD: Scalp - Wounds Ears, Nose - Fluid Eyes - Pupils Jaw - Stability Mouth - Wounds		
NECK: Wounds, Deformity		
CHEST: Wounds, Deformity		
ABDOMEN: Wounds, Rigidity		
BACK: Wounds, Deformity		
PELVIS: Stability, Pain		
EXTREMITIES: Wounds, Deformity Sensation & Movement Pulses Below Injury		
LOOK FOR MEDICAL ID TAG		
VICTIM'S NAME		AGE
COMPLETED BY		

IN CLASS VERSION

RESCUE REQUEST

Fill Out One Form Per Victim

TIME OF INCIDENT		Date
AM PM		

NATURE OF INCIDENT
FALL: — Rock — Snow — Crevasse — Avalanche

— ILLNESS EXCESSIVE: — Heat — Cold

BRIEF DESCRIPTION OF INCIDENT

INJURIES (List most severe first)	FIRST AID GIVEN
SKIN TEMP/COLOR	
STATE OF CONSCIOUSNESS	
PAIN (Location)	

RECORD

Time Pulse Respiration					

VICTIM'S NAME AGE

ADDRESS

NOTIFY (Name)

RELATIONSHIP	PHONE

SIDE 2 RESCUE REQUEST

EXACT LOCATION (Include Marked Map If Possible)

QUADRANGLE: SECTION:

AREA DESCRIPTION
TERRAIN: __ GLACIER   __ SNOW   __ ROCK

__ BRUSH   __ TIMBER   __ TRAIL

__ FLAT   __ MODERATE   __ STEEP

ON-SITE PLANS
__ Will Stay Put
__ Will Evacuate to _____

Can Stay Overnight Safely: __ Yes __ No
On-Site Equipment: __ Tent __ Stove __ Food

__ Ground Insulation __ Flare   __ CB Radio
LOCAL WEATHER

EVACUATION:
__ Carry-Out __ Helicopter __ Lowering __ Raising

EQUIPMENT: __ Rigid Litter __ Food __ Water __ Other

PARTY MEMBERS REMAINING

_____ Beginners   _____ Intermediate   _____ Experienced

NAME   NOTIFY (Name)   PHONE

NOTIFY: IN NATIONAL PARK: Ranger
        OUTSIDE NATIONAL PARK: Sheriff/County Police
        RCMP (Canada)

VITAL SIGN RECORD

Record TIME	BREATHS		PULSE		PULSES BELOW INJURY	PUPILS	SKIN	STATE OF CONSCIOUS-NESS	Other
	rate	character	rate	character					
		deep shallow noisy labored		strong weak regular irregular	strong weak absent	equal round reactive to light	color temp moistness	alert confused unresponsive	pain, anxiety thirst, etc

About the Authors

Jan Carline became interested in mountaineering first aid after he learned, the hard way, the hazards of walking up a Cascade mountain trail in April while wearing tennis shoes. He has been affiliated with the Mountaineering Oriented First Aid (MOFA) program for over fifteen years and is currently an instructor and trainer of MOFA instructors. Carline has served as chairman of several activities committees of The Mountaineers, including first aid, safety, and non-technical climbing, and has been chairman of the Health Services Committee of the Seattle–King County Chapter of the American Red Cross. In his free time, Carline is a faculty member in Medical Education at the University of Washington, specializing in the evaluation of student performance and the improvement of teaching.

Martha J. Lentz, Ph.D., R.N., is a faculty member of the University of Washington School of Nursing, with experience in both orthopedic and emergency nursing. Lentz has been active in the MOFA program for the past twenty-five years as an instructor and instructor trainer. She is a graduate of The Mountaineers basic and intermediate climbing courses. As a member of the Seattle Mountain Rescue she has participated in mountain rescues in the Cascade Mountains. Lentz is also active in biking and sea kayaking.

Steven C. Macdonald is a graduate of The Mountaineers scrambling, Alpine winter travel (snowshoeing), and basic mountaineering courses. He has worked on ambulances, trained Emergency Medical Technicians, conducted research in preventive medicine, and completed fellowships in environmental pathology and toxicology, and health policy research. Macdonald received his Ph.D. from the University of Washington School of Public Health. He has worked as an epidemiologist in the National Center for Environmental Health at the federal Centers for Disease Control & Prevention in Atlanta, and currently works in the Office of Epidemiology at the Washington State Department of Health. Macdonald has taught the MOFA course and has been active in the Seattle Mountaineers MOFA Committee.

THE MOUNTAINEERS, founded in 1906, is a nonprofit outdoor activity and conservation club, whose mission is "to explore, study, preserve, and enjoy the natural beauty of the outdoors. . . . " Based in Seattle, Washington, the club is now the third-largest such organization in the United States, with seven branches throughout Washington State.

The Mountaineers sponsors both classes and year-round outdoor activities in the Pacific Northwest, which include hiking, mountain climbing, ski-touring, snowshoeing, bicycling, camping, kayaking, nature study, sailing, and adventure travel. The club's conservation division supports environmental causes through educational activities, sponsoring legislation, and presenting informational programs.

All club activities are led by skilled, experienced instructors, who are dedicated to promoting safe and responsible enjoyment and preservation of the outdoors.

If you would like to participate in these organized outdoor activities or the club's programs, consider a membership in The Mountaineers. For information and an application, write or call The Mountaineers, Club Headquarters, 300 Third Avenue West, Seattle, WA 98119; 206-284-6310. You can also visit the club's website at *www.mountaineers.org* or contact The Mountaineers via email at *clubmail@mountaineers.org*.

The Mountaineers Books, an active, nonprofit publishing program of the club, produces guidebooks, instructional texts, historical works, natural history guides, and works on environmental conservation. All books produced by The Mountaineers Books fulfill the club's mission.

Send or call for our catalog of more than 500 outdoor titles:

The Mountaineers Books
1001 SW Klickitat Way, Suite 201
Seattle, WA 98134
800-553-4453
mbooks@mountaineersbooks.org
www.mountaineersbooks.org

The Mountaineers Books is proud to be a corporate sponsor of The Leave No Trace Center for Outdoor Ethics, whose mission is to promote and inspire responsible outdoor recreation through education, research, and partnerships. The Leave No Trace program is focused specifically on human-powered (nonmotorized) recreation.

Leave No Trace strives to educate visitors about the nature of their recreational impacts, as well as offer techniques to prevent and minimize such impacts. Leave No Trace is best understood as an educational and ethical program, not as a set of rules and regulations.

For more information, visit *www.LNT.org*, or call 800-332-4100.

ALSO IN THE MOUNTAINEERS OUTDOOR BASICS SERIES

Wilderness Navigation: Finding Your Way Using Map, Compass, Altimeter, & GPS, *Bob & Mike Burns*
A classic handbook for learning to navigate—extensively updated to include the newest trends and devices

Wilderness Basics
San Diego chapter of The Sierra Club
A classic handbook for the outdoor novice interested in hiking, backpacking, paddling, and mountain biking

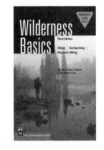

The Outdoor Knots Book
Clyde Soles
A guide to the ropes and knots used in the outdoors by hikers, campers, paddlers, and climbers.

OTHER TITLES YOU MIGHT ENJOY FROM THE MOUNTAINEERS BOOKS

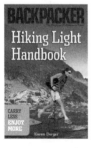

Don't Forget the Duct Tape: Tips and Tricks for Emergency Gear Repair, *Kristin Hostetter*
Pack this little guide with you and be an outdoor fixit guru!

Conditioning for Outdoor Fitness: Functional Exercise & Nutrition for Everyone, *David Musnick, M.D. and Mark Pierce, A.T.C.*
The bestselling book on fitness for outdoor sports

Hiking Light Handbook
Karen Berger
Practical, reasonable strategies for everyone who'd like to lighten their load on the trail.

Available at fine bookstores and outdoor stores, by phone at 800-553-4453 or on the web at *www.mountaineersbooks.org*

THE MOUNTAINEERS BOOKS